Past Masters
General Editor   Keith Thomas

Leibniz

George MacDonald Ross is Senior Lecturer in
Philosophy and Head of Department at the
University of Leeds, and is currently working on
a translation of some of Leibniz's Latin corres-
pondence. His most recent publication, with Tony
McWalter, is *Kant and His Influence*.

Past Masters

AQUINAS Anthony Kenny
ARISTOTLE Jonathan Barnes
AUGUSTINE Henry Chadwick
BENTHAM John Dinwiddy
THE BUDDHA Michael Carrithers
CLAUSEWITZ Michael Howard
COLERIDGE Richard Holmes
DARWIN Jonathan Howard
DESCARTES Tom Sorell
DISRAELI John Vincent
DURKHEIM Frank Parkin
GEORGE ELIOT Rosemary Ashton
ENGELS Terrell Carver
ERASMUS James McConica
FREUD Anthony Storr
GALILEO Stillman Drake
GOETHE T. J. Reed
HEGEL Peter Singer
HOBBES Richard Tuck
HOMER Jasper Griffin
HUME A. J. Ayer
JESUS Humphrey Carpenter
JOHNSON Pat Rogers
JUNG Anthony Stevens
KANT Roger Scruton
KEYNES Robert Skidelsky
KIERKEGAARD Patrick Gardiner

LEIBNIZ G. MacDonald Ross
LOCKE John Dunn
MACHIAVELLI Quentin Skinner
MALTHUS Donald Winch
MARX Peter Singer
MONTAIGNE Peter Burke
MONTESQUIEU Judith N. Shklar
THOMAS MORE Anthony Kenny
MUHAMMAD Michael Cook
NEWMAN Owen Chadwick
NIETZSCHE Michael Tanner
PAINE Mark Philp
PAUL E. P. Sanders
PLATO R. M. Hare
ROUSSEAU Robert Wokler
RUSSELL A. C. Grayling
SCHILLER T. J. Reed
SCHOPENHAUER Christopher
  Janaway
SHAKESPEARE Germaine Greer
ADAM SMITH D. D. Raphael
SPINOZA Roger Scruton
TOCQUEVILLE Larry Siedentop
VICO Peter Burke
VIRGIL Jasper Griffin
WITTGENSTEIN A. C. Grayling

Forthcoming

JOSEPH BUTLER R. G. Frey
COPERNICUS Owen Gingerich
GANDHI Bhikhu Parekh
HEIDEGGER Michael Inwood

SOCRATES C. C. W. Taylor
WEBER Peter Ghosh
and others

G. MacDonald Ross

Leibniz

Oxford   New York

OXFORD UNIVERSITY PRESS

Oxford University Press, Great Clarendon Street, Oxford OX2 6DP

Oxford New York

Athens Auckland Bangkok Bogota Buenos Aires Calcutta
Cape Town Chennai Dar es Salaam Delhi Florence Hong Kong Istanbul
Karachi Kuala Lumpur Madrid Melbourne Mexico City Mumbai
Nairobi Paris São Paolo Singapore Taipei Tokyo Toronto Warsaw

and associated companies in
Berlin Ibadan

Oxford is a registered trade mark of Oxford University Press

First published 1984 as an Oxford University Press paperback
and simultaneously in a hardback edition
Reissued 1996

British Library Cataloguing in Publication Data
Data available

ISBN 0-19-287620-1

10 9 8 7 6

Printed in Great Britain by
Cox & Wyman Ldd,
Reading, Berkshire

Contents

Abbreviations *vi*

Introduction *1*

1 Life and character *3*

2 Mathematics *28*

3 Science *37*

4 Logic *49*

5 Metaphysics *73*

6 God and man *101*

7 Influence *113*

Further reading *116*

Index *118*

Abbreviations

All the quotations are my own translations. I have not specified any particular edition for the *Monadology*, which is included in most collections, and is referred to here by paragragh in the normal way. The rest are from the following editions:

C *Opuscules et fragments inédits de Leibniz* [Unpublished Short Works and Fragments of Leibniz], ed. Louis Couturat (Paris, 1903)

D *God. Guil. Leibnitii Opera Omnia* [Leibniz's Complete Works], ed. Louis Dutens, 6 vols, (Geneva, 1768)

E *God. Guil. Leibnitii opera philosophica quae extant* [Leibniz's Extant Philosophical Works], ed. Johann E. Erdmann, 2 vols in one (Berlin, 1840)

G *Leibniz, G. W., Die Philosophischen Schriften* [The Philosophical Writings], ed. C. I. Gerhard, 7 vols, (Berlin, 1875-90)

S *Leibniz' Deutsche Schriften* [Leibniz's German Writings], ed. G. E. Guhrauer, 2 vols, (Berlin, 1838-40)

Introduction

Traditionally, university courses on the history of modern philosophy have been structured round a pantheon of seven great philosophers: three 'continental rationalists': Descartes, Spinoza and Leibniz; three 'British empiricists': Locke, Berkeley and Hume; and Kant. The empiricists were supposed to have believed that all our knowledge was built up out of the data of sense, whereas the rationalists were supposed to have restricted genuine knowledge to what could be deduced from indubitable truths of reason. Kant, on the other hand, created a new synthesis out of what was right in both empiricism and rationalism. Needless to say, this way of viewing the history of philosophy was invented by Kant himself. It has, however, had a remarkably long run for its money.

Historians of philosophy have always found particular difficulty in forcing Leibniz into this Kantian mould, since his approach was markedly less rationalist than that of either Descartes or Spinoza. During the present century, there has been a growing tendency among professional philosophers to see logic as central to their discipline. Consequently the focus of interest in Leibniz's thought has shifted to his work on formal logic, and the extent to which his philosophy can be interpreted as derived from his logic. However, this approach leaves many questions unanswered, and commentators have been positively embarrassed by the many quirkier aspects of Leibniz's philosophical work. These obviously have nothing to do with logic.

In fact, Leibniz stood on the interface between the holistic and vitalist world-view of the Renaissance, and the atomistic and mechanistic materialism that was to dominate the eighteenth and nineteenth centuries. As we shall see, many of his ideas were too radical for his own age, and were taken up only much later – sometimes not until the present century. It would be rash to judge him merely by those ideas which have subsequently become part of our view of the world. As with all great philosophers, his work no doubt contains hitherto unrecognised potential.

Another common distortion is to see Leibniz as primarily a *philosopher*, as if his role in life were the same as that of the twentieth-century professional philosopher. Not only was he never employed as a professor of philosophy, but the range of his interests was so wide that his philosophical work was no more than one activity among many. He was, as the Germans quite rightly call him, an *Universalgenie* – a 'universal genius'. A balanced account of his achievement must place his philosophy in the context of everything else he did. Only then is it possible to appreciate how Leibniz, far from being the extreme 'rationalist' Kant made him out to be, was really himself aiming to create a new synthesis out of the apparently irreconcilable conflicts between earlier traditions in various spheres of intellectual activity.

1 Life and character

Early years (1646–67)

Gottfried Wilhelm von Leibniz was born in Leipzig, on Sunday 1 July 1646. His father, Friedrich Leibnütz (1597–1652), was Professor of Moral Philosophy at Leipzig University. His mother, Catherina Schmuck (1621–64), was Friedrich's third wife. Leibniz had a half-brother Johann Friedrich (d. 1696), and a sister Anna Catherina (1648–72), whose son Friedrich Simon Löffler was eventually his sole heir. During his twenties, Leibniz changed the spelling of his name from '-ütz' to '-iz': he himself never used the '-itz' form, which became the normal spelling during his own lifetime, and which has only recently gone out of fashion.

Little is known about Leibniz's early education, beyond what he tells us in incidental reminiscences, which probably exaggerate the extent to which he was self-taught. He learned to read from his father, well before going to school at the age of seven. He claims that he taught himself Latin from an illustrated Livy, and that by the age of eight he was avidly reading his late father's books. It is hard to imagine what he can have made of them at first, since he was not fluent in Latin until the age of twelve, and was only then beginning Greek. But they certainly formed the basis of his later massive erudition in the classics, the Church Fathers, and scholastic philosophy. On top of this, his school syllabus was itself very demanding, including German literature and history, Latin, Greek, theology and logic. This last was of particular interest to him, and at the age of thirteen he was already trying to improve on the Aristotelian theory of the categories, despite discouragement from his teachers.

Leibniz moved on to Leipzig University after Easter 1661, when he was still only fourteen (young, but not exceptionally so in those days). He followed the standard two-year arts course, which included philosophy, rhetoric, mathematics, Latin, Greek and Hebrew. After graduating, he could proceed only by studying for a doctorate in one of the 'higher' faculties of Theology, Law, or Medicine. He opted for Law, but before starting his course, he spent the short summer term at the nearby university of Jena. Here he came into contact with more unorthodox ideas, in particular Erhard Weigel's Neopythagoreanism, according to which Number is the fundamental reality of the universe.

Following his return to Leipzig, Leibniz spent the next three years working at a series of 'disputations' which he had to publish and defend in open debate at each stage (or 'degree') of his student career. In addition to bachelor's and master's disputations in law, in his final year he wrote a *Dissertation on the Art of Combinations*, by which he 'habilitated', that is, became qualified to lecture in philosophy. However, he did not exercise his right to teach philosophy, since such lectureships were purely honorary, and he was already heavily in debt to his relatives. Rather, he had his eyes on one of twelve established law tutorships, which went to doctors of law whenever vacancies occurred, in order of date of graduation. Unfortunately, there were too many doctoral candidates that year, and the younger ones, including Leibniz, were told to wait until a later degree day. He took this very badly, and suspected a conspiracy directed against him personally by the Dean's wife, for motives which he never explained. So he moved on to the little university of Altdorf, just outside Nuremberg, which was then a major centre of science and technology. Almost as soon as he had registered (4 October 1666), he submitted his already prepared doctoral thesis, and was formally awarded the degree the following February. He so impressed the Altdorf academics, that he was offered a professorship; but by that time he had changed his mind about an academic career, and decided instead to become more involved in the outside world.

Alchemist, jurist and polymath (1667–72)

Leibniz's first job was a stopgap, and he may already have had it while still officially a student at Altdorf. It was the secretaryship of a society of Nuremberg intellectuals interested in alchemy (not Rosicrucians, as has often been asserted). It is unclear what his duties were – on alchemical questions Leibniz consistently adhered to the tradition of secretiveness. In contrast with his contemporary Isaac Newton, it is unlikely that he ever did any actual laboratory work, but he certainly acquired a reputation as an adept with deep theoretical understanding of the art. To his dying day he retained a close interest in alchemy (he talked about it with his doctor on his death-bed), and he periodically arranged tests of the claims of various alchemists. His declared motives were scientific: if transmutation were a practical possibility, the process should yield valuable information about the structure of matter. But in fact he also hoped to make his fortune from it. Thus, in about 1676, he entered into a formal profit-sharing agreement with two practising alchemists (G. H. Schuller and J. D. Crafft), his side of the bargain being to provide capital and technical advice: he was always a soft touch for people wanting to borrow money for alchemical experiments. His main reservation about gold-making was that gold would lose its value if it could be made too cheaply.

Whatever his precise relationship with the Nuremberg alchemists, he did not stay with them for long. Sometime during the summer he was on the move again, intending to travel 'to Holland and beyond'. By chance he met up with Baron Johann Christian von Boineburg, the former chief minister of the Elector of Mainz, Johann Philipp von Schönborn. Impressed by Leibniz's alchemical erudition, as well as by his obvious employability in state service, Boineburg persuaded him to accept his patronage, and go home with him to Frankfurt-am-Main, just outside Mainz. Boineburg soon managed to get him appointed as assistant to the Elector's legal adviser, who was working on a recodification of civil law. About a year and a half later, Leibniz was promoted to the rank of Assessor in the Court of Appeal.

Despite this appointment, he was still very much Boineburg's protégé, and for the next five years he spent as much time in Frankfurt as in Mainz. Leibniz's close relationship with Boineburg was important, not merely for launching him on his career, but also at an intellectual and personal level. In particular, Boineburg and other members of his circle were converts from Lutheranism to Catholicism. Leibniz very nearly followed their example, and it says much for his sincerity that in later years, when offered the prestigious librarianships of the Vatican (in 1689), of Paris (in 1698), and perhaps also of Vienna, he turned them down only because he was not prepared to go through a formal conversion. However, despite his loyalty to Lutheranism, he moved easily in Catholic circles, and was ideally placed to further the reunification of the churches, which was one of his life's ambitions. With Boineburg's encouragement, he drafted a number of monographs on religious topics, mostly to do with points at issue between the churches, such as the doctrine of transubstantiation.

As we shall see in Chapter 4, one of the corner-stones of Leibniz's philosophy was his vision of a 'universal encyclopaedia', which would incorporate all knowledge into a single system. Many of his activities were intended as contributions towards this long-term goal, including his employment on legal recodification at Mainz, since he believed that natural law constituted a proper part of human knowledge.

As it stood, German law comprised a chaotic mixture of the Roman code, traditional Germanic common law, and the statute and case law of the various states. Leibniz hoped to reduce it to order by defining all legal concepts in terms of a few basic ones, and deducing all specific laws from a small set of incontrovertible principles of natural justice. Among his papers there survive many draft attempts at such a system, and he published a number of short treatises on the topic during his Mainz period (for example, the *New Method of Teaching and Learning Jurisprudence* of 1667). Although the focus of his interests moved away from law as he got older, he kept on returning to this youthful project. However, not only was it a huge task to reduce the whole of *natural* law to a system, but he never began to solve the problem of extending it to *civil* legislation.

More generally, Leibniz's scheme for a universal encyclopaedia required a pooling of existing knowledge, of research in hand, and of future efforts. There had already been attempts to encompass all knowledge in a single work, for example J. H. Alsted's seven-volume *Encyclopaedia* of 1630, which Leibniz once thought of adapting to his own purposes. But the vast bulk of current knowledge was in books scattered throughout the libraries of Europe, and he soon saw that the most feasible way of centralising access to it would be to compile a master subject-catalogue. At the time the only useful subject-catalogue in existence was that of the Bodleian Library at Oxford, and Leibniz had no knowledge of it. In 1670 he produced as a model a catalogue of Boineburg's rich book collection; but despite repeated pleas, he was never allowed to do the same for any of the major libraries which were later in his charge, and only recently has his dream of the librarian as specialist in information storage and retrieval again been taken up by professional librarians.

As for setting up a central register of new discoveries, Leibniz devised a scheme for a review of books, which he called a *nucleus librarius*, to include abstracts of all new serious publications. His long-term plan was to expand it to cover earlier publications, unpublished works, research in progress, and a cumulative subject-index. Twice he applied for the necessary imperial licence (in 1668 and 1669), but on each occasion he was turned down, presumably because of fears that it would harm the retail book trade. However, despite the failure of the more grandiose scheme, he continued to do what he could in the same general direction. Throughout his life he kept a card-index of all the important books he read (an immense number); he was a regular contributor to such review journals as existed (notably the *Journal des Sçavans*, founded in 1665, and the *Acta Eruditorum*, founded in 1682); and much later, in 1700, he started his own journal, the *Monatliche Auszug*, under the editorship of his assistant Johann Georg von Eckhart. This, however, folded after only two years.

The need to co-ordinate research naturally suggested the foundation of learned and scientific societies. Like many of his contemporaries, Leibniz dreamed up various utopian schemes for communes of researchers, and he also proposed exhibitions and museums for popularising and funding science. Until he was influential enough for his plans to have any real chance of success, the only practical step was for him to join such societies as already existed. With this in mind, he composed a number of treatises on scientific topics, two of which he had printed with dedications to the Royal Society of London, and to the Paris Academy. He was elected to the former on 19 April 1673, but he had to wait until 13 March 1700 to be made an external member of the latter.

Although scientific societies and periodicals were gradually coming into existence during the seventeenth century, by far the most important medium of intellectual co-operation and dissemination of ideas was the exchange of letters. These were often widely distributed among the acquaintances of the correspondents, and it was also common for collections of such letters to be published in book form. For example, in 1697 Leibniz published a selection from his correspondence, mainly with Jesuit missionaries, about China, under the title *Novissima Sinica* ('The Latest from China'). Boineburg was an avid letter-writer, and he helped Leibniz to build up his own circle of correspondents by putting him in touch with intellectuals from all over Europe. Within a few years, Leibniz was in correspondence with literally hundreds of people at a time on almost every subject under the sun – science, mathematics, law, politics, religion, philosophy, literature, history, linguistics, numismatics, anthropology. He was obsessive about preserving his letters, and over 15,000 still survive. It is on these, and on a comparable mass of private notes and drafts, that we rely for most of our knowledge of his work, especially in the areas of philosophy, logic and mathematics. As he once wrote, 'Anyone who knows me only by my publications does not know me at all' (D vi i 65). Most of the manuscript material is in Latin, which was still (though not for much longer) the lingua franca of the scholarly world. He often corresponded in French (even with fellow Germans), but hardly ever in German. When he did, he frequently lapsed into Latin because of the lack of abstract technical terms in German. As a keen nationalist he much regretted the fact, and proposed a German Academy to enrich and promote the German language. He occasionally tried to write philosophy in a German free of Latinate borrowings, very much in the spirit of the largely successful eighteenth-century movement for linguistic purity.

Although Leibniz's interests were clearly developing in a scientific direction, he still hankered after a literary career. All his life he prided himself on his poetry (mostly Latin), and boasted that he could recite the bulk of Virgil's *Aeneid* by heart. During his time with Boineburg he would have passed for a typical late Renaissance humanist. His Latin style was still elaborate and florid, he never missed any opportunity to parade his classical learning, and his principal publication was an edition of the *Antibarbarus* of the sixteenth-century Italian humanist Mario Nizolio. Leibniz was broadly sympathetic with Nizolio's theme, which was that a pure style in Latin was a surer route to knowledge and wisdom than the logic and linguistic barbarism of university philosophy. In 1673 Leibniz promised to do the Delphin Classics edition of Martianus Capella (the fifth-century author of a fantastic allegory on the seven liberal arts), but he never got round to it. In 1676 he translated Plato's *Phaedo* and *Theaetetus* into Latin, and was the first modern scholar to detect a sharp contrast between the philosophy of the historical Plato, and the mystical and superstitious 'Neoplatonism' (or 'Pseudo-Platonism', as Leibniz called it) of Plato's later followers.

Leibniz also applied his mind to political questions. For example, soon after his arrival in Mainz, he published a short treatise using deductive arguments to solve the question of the Polish succession. A more long-standing problem was the French threat to Germany, now seriously weakened by the Thirty Years War. Leibniz periodically came up with anti-French ideas, such as undercutting the brandy trade with cheap rum from West Indian sugar; and in 1684 he published an anonymous satire on Louis XIV's bellicosity, under the title *Mars Christianissimus* (Mars being the god of war, and Louis being known as *Rex Christianissimus*, 'The Most Christian King'). While still under Boineburg's patronage, he devised a plan to distract Louis away from Northern Europe with an enticing scheme for a French conquest of Egypt (the strategy he suggested was almost identical to the one actually carried out by Napoleon a century and a half later). Boineburg was so impressed by the plan, that he arranged for Leibniz to go to Paris to try and lay it before the French government.

Paris (1672–6)

On arriving in Paris in the spring of 1672, and while waiting for an opportunity to carry out his political objective, Leibniz set about getting himself known in intellectual circles. He soon had a wide range of acquaintances, including the philosophers Arnauld and Malebranche, and the mathematician Huygens. Through his philosophical contacts, he managed to get access to the unpublished writings of the two greatest French philosophers of the previous generation, Pascal and Descartes, and some of the latter survive only through the copies he himself made. As we shall see, his close but critical study of Descartes' work was one of the major influences on his mature philosophical system. But at this stage, his main interest was in mathematics. Because of the narrowness of his mathematical education in backward Germany, he had arrived in Paris with exaggerated ideas of his own achievements. After a number of embarrassing encounters with various leading mathematicians, mainly French and English, he was forced to realise that he still had a lot to learn. Far from being discouraged, he immersed himself in mathematical studies under the guidance of Huygens, and by the time he left Paris he had already made most of the discoveries that were to earn him his leading place in the history of the subject.

But Leibniz's official reason for being in Paris came to nothing: he never found an opportunity to present his Egyptian plan to the King. In November 1672, Boineburg sent his son Philipp Wilhelm to Paris to finish his education under Leibniz's charge. He arrived in the company of his brother-in-law, the Elector's nephew Melchior Friedrich von Schönborn, who was on a diplomatic mission. This meant that Leibniz had both continued financial support, and the status of a semi-official attaché. Most importantly, he took part in a trip to London, in January 1673, which enabled him to make personal contact with members of the Royal Society, in particular its secretary, his fellow German Henry Oldenburg. The Society had given a mixed reception to his treatise, *The Theory of Concrete Motion*, which he had sent them (see p. 8 above), but they were very intrigued by another of his projects which he had brought along to show them. This was the prototype of a mechanical calculator he had been working on while still in Germany.

He was very proud of his invention. He once thought of commemorating it with a medal bearing the motto SUPERIOR TO MAN, and much later he had a machine made for Peter the Great of Russia to send to the Emperor of China as an example of superior Western technology. Its immediate applications were obvious: it would save considerable labour and improve accuracy in accountancy, administration, surveying, scientific research, production of mathematical tables and so on. This was all more significant than we might now appreciate, since at the time even educated people rarely understood multiplication, let alone division (Pepys had to learn his multiplication tables when already a senior administrator). For the long term, he envisaged a larger version of his calculator being used to mechanise *all* reasoning processes, once all possible thoughts had been given a number through his projected 'Universal Characteristic' (see Chapter 4 below). Instead of fruitless arguing, people would say, 'Let us calculate' – and they could do so by setting the dials and cranking the handle of his machine (one of a number of Leibnizian schemes satirised in Swift's *Voyage to Balnibarbi*).

The calculator itself was a considerable advance on earlier adding machines, such as Wilhelm Schickard's of 1623, or Pascal's of 1642. Leibniz designed it specifically as a multiplier and divider, and invented a number of devices which became standard in later technology – in particular the stepped reckoner (or 'Leibniz wheel'), which had cogs of varying lengths. However, despite spending a small fortune on the project right up to the end of his life, he never developed a version which could do carrying completely automatically. One of his models still survives, and is now in the Hanover State Library.

While in Paris, Leibniz was full of other technological ideas. The one he had most fully worked out was a watch with two symmetrical balance wheels working in tandem, of which he demonstrated a model to the Paris Academy in April 1675. Others were a device for calculating a ship's position without using a compass or observing the stars, a method for determining the distance of an object from a single observation point, a compressed-air engine for propelling vehicles or projectiles, a ship which could go under water to escape enemy detection (though he rejected space flight on the grounds that the air would be too thin), an aneroid barometer (subsequently reinvented by Vidi of Paris in 1843), and various improvements to the design of lenses.

Leibniz's trip to London was cut short by the news of the sudden deaths of both his patrons: of Boineburg in December 1672, and of the Elector in February 1673. He arrived back in Paris in early March, but continued as the young Boineburg's tutor till his appointment came to an end in September 1674. He was now twenty-eight, but despite his acknowledged brilliance, he had no settled career. Although he had been offered jobs at the courts of Hanover and of Denmark, what he really wanted was a research post attached to the Paris Academy. Eventually he was forced to recognise that no such position was forthcoming, and since he was running seriously into debt, he reluctantly accepted the post of Court Councillor at Hanover. His appointment was officially from January 1676, but he managed to delay his arrival until December of that year. He left Paris in October, and took a roundabout route via London and Holland. His stay in London was very brief. In Amsterdam he got to know the pioneering microscopist Antonie van Leeuwenhoek, who had recently made the first observations of bacteria, protozoa and spermatozoa. Leibniz also had four days of intense discussions with the famous lens-grinder and philosopher, Benedict de Spinoza at the Hague.

Librarian and mining engineer (1676–86)

The administration at Hanover was typical of that of the hundred or so independent states under the titular leadership of the German Emperor in Vienna. The autocratic head of state, in this case Duke Johann Friedrich of Brunswick-Lüneburg, acted through a council composed largely of lesser aristocrats and law graduates, some of whom were delegated more specialist functions. Leibniz managed to negotiate partial relief from normal council duties because of the burden of his particular responsibilities as librarian, political adviser, international correspondent and, increasingly, as technological adviser.

His duties as librarian were onerous, but fairly mundane: general administration, purchase of new books and second-hand libraries, and conventional cataloguing. In 1679 he had to cope with the transfer of the library from the suburban Herrenhausen palace to Hanover itself, and two years later with its removal to more extensive accommodation in a rear wing. From 1698 it was housed in a separate building, with living quarters for the librarian. (The *'Leibniz-Haus'* was destroyed in World War II, but a replica was inaugurated in 1983.) In 1690 Leibniz also undertook overall responsibility for the much more prestigious *Bibliotheca Augusta* at Wolfenbüttel, about 70 kilometres south-east of Hanover. He was expressly forbidden to reorganise it along the lines of any of his pet schemes, but he was at least able to oversee the drawing up of a main-entry alphabetical author catalogue. In 1705 the books were removed to the armoury while a grand new library was being built. Unfortunately, many of Leibniz's sensible suggestions for it (such as the provision of lighting and heating) were ignored, and the building did not come into commission until after his death. His problems with the library were further exacerbated by the appointment, also in 1705, of a deputy librarian with whom he was perpetually at loggerheads.

Throughout this period of his career, Leibniz's principal efforts were directed towards technological innovation. He seems to have spent much time in conclave with the Duke (as also with his successor) discussing alchemical recipes and testing the claims of itinerant alchemists. Among the alchemists he got to know at this time were J. D. Crafft (see p. 5) and J. J. Becher. He remained a close friend of Crafft for many years, but he soon fell out with Becher. Leibniz had put a stop to one of Becher's more idiotic alchemical schemes, and in revenge Becher satirised him in his book *Foolish Wisdom and Wise Folly*, for claiming to have invented a coach which could travel from Amsterdam to Hanover in six hours (i.e.

about 60 k.p.h. on deeply rutted cart-tracks). We know that they did discuss coach design in 1678, and that then and later Leibniz did have interesting ideas for increasing speed, in particular for reducing friction by something like a system of ball-bearings. He even had a coach built to his own design in 1697, although unfortunately we know nothing of its technical details. Considering how far-fetched some of Leibniz's ideas were, it may be that Becher's report was not so exaggerated. The speed suggested is not much faster than that of a modern racing bicycle, and Leibniz may have envisaged the use of a compressed-air or steam engine (such as that of the French inventor Denis Papin (1647–1714), for which he once suggested an improved self-regulating mechanism).

It was through Crafft that Leibniz came into contact with another German alchemist, Heinrich Brand, the discoverer of phosphorus. It seems that Brand was working from an old alchemical text which hinted that the philosopher's stone was to be found in the dregs of the human body. He took this literally, tried distilling urine, and produced phosphorus. Quite apart from the possibility of its being a step towards the philosopher's stone, it had considerable commercial value as a curiosity for the then fashionable courtly scientific demonstrations, and potential as a weapon of war. In 1678, Leibniz managed to engage Brand to the services of Hanover with an exclusive contract. From Brand's point of view, he had the advantage of virtually unlimited supplies of urine from the workers' latrines in the Duchy's mines in the Harz mountains, about 100 kilometres south-east of Hanover.

At the same time, Leibniz became obsessed by the problem of draining water from the Harz mines. Early in 1679 he conceived the idea of using wind power, and he persuaded the Duke to let him try various experiments, with a handsome life pension if he succeeded. From then until the end of 1686 he spent more than half his time in the Harz mountains. He designed all sorts of windmills, gearing mechanisms and pumps, which included Archimedean screws, syphons, compressed-air power links and even a forerunner of the modern rotary pump. He also proposed the replacing of pit ponies by water power, new designs for ore-carriers, improved methods of casting iron and manufacturing steel, and a technique for separating chemicals and desalinating water.

As far as we know, every single one of these projects ended in failure. Leibniz himself believed that this was because of deliberate obstruction by administrators and technicians, and the workers' fears that technological progress would cost them their jobs. He certainly did face repeated attacks in the Court Council – not entirely unjustified, since his over-ambitious and often half-baked schemes must have caused considerable expense and disruption of normal working. It says much for the patience of successive Dukes that Leibniz's interference was tolerated as long as it was. Quite apart from the Harz mines, he kept on submitting memoranda on all sorts of technical projects, such as canals, inland navigation, water supply, fountains for the Herrenhausen palace gardens, linen production, porcelain manufacture, exploitation of waste heat in chimneys; and also on socio-political issues such as monetary policy, tax reform, balance of trade, and a primitive national insurance scheme.

Historian and archivist (1687-97)

Duke Johann Friedrich had died in December 1679, his successor being his younger brother Ernst August. In order to further his dynastic ambitions by establishing and publicising the historical rights of the House of Brunswick, Ernst August had suggested to Leibniz that he carry out research for a book on its recent history. Nothing much came of this at the time, since Leibniz had barely started on his involvement with the Harz mines. But by August 1685 it was evident that the drainage experiments were a failure. Perhaps primarily as a means of getting him away from the mines, Ernst August contracted him to write a history of the whole Guelf family, of which the House of Brunswick was a branch. It was to run from earliest times to the present, and Leibniz was guaranteed a permanent salary for the project. Even so, it was not until December 1686 that he finally left the Harz, and started on serious historical research.

He soon exhausted the archival material available locally, and was given permission for a long trip to Bavaria, Austria and Italy. He was away from November 1687 to June 1690. Apart from his archival work, he took the opportunity to get to know many more scholars and scientists, and was elected a member of the Physico-Mathematical Academy of Rome. He had many discussions on church unity, and in Vienna he made an impression on the Emperor, Leopold I, though not enough to get him a post as Imperial Councillor and Official Historian, or permission to set up a 'universal library'. About the same time he completed his first successful diplomatic mission, which was to negotiate the marriage of Duke Johann Friedrich's daughter Charlotte Felicitas to the Duke of Modena.

On returning to Hanover, Leibniz set about improving his position by acquiring part-time appointments at other courts ruled by branches of the Brunswick family. It was then that he was given charge of the *Bibliotheca Augusta* at Wolfenbüttel by the co-Dukes Rudolf August and Anton Ulrich of Brunswick-Wolfenbüttel. They also agreed to pay a third of the costs of publishing the Guelf history, much of the material for which was in their library. Early in 1691, Duke Georg Wilhelm of Celle, Ernst August's brother, also gave Leibniz an allowance for his historical work. A few years later, in 1696, he was promoted to Privy Councillor at Brunswick-Wolfenbüttel. His salaries were now 1,000 thalers a year from Hanover, 400 from Brunswick-Wolfenbüttel, and 200 from Celle, of which even the lowest was more than a skilled worker could hope to earn (the thaler was worth about five English shillings). For the rest of his life, he was to be in Brunswick, Wolfenbüttel and Celle almost as much as in Hanover itself. The round trip was some 200 kilometres, and a lot of his time was spent travelling. Although he had his own coach, it is nevertheless remarkable that he managed to write letters while on the move (and understandable that he was so interested in improving coach design).

Despite repeated complaints from his various employers that he was doing everything but what he was being paid for, Leibniz did a considerable amount of work on the history of the Guelfs. As a preliminary to the history itself, he edited a vast mass of mostly unpublished archival material. He published six enormous volumes in 1698–1700, and a further three relating specifically to the Guelfs (the *Scriptores rerum Brunsvicensium*) in 1707–11. More saw the light of day after his death. He also completed two preliminary essays which show how literally he took the commission to start from earliest times. The first was called *Protogaea*, about the formation of minerals and fossils, and depending mainly on observations made in the Harz; the second was about European tribal migrations, as inferred from linguistic and place-name evidence. He collected an enormous amount of information about the origins of European languages, primarily in order to find evidence for a single archetypal language (Hebrew, perhaps), although his actual findings led him to conclude that different language groups had separate origins. More specifically, he disproved the claim of certain Swedish scholars that

Swedish was the oldest, and therefore the noblest of European languages.

Among the side-products of his archival work in Italy was a detailed refutation, not published in his lifetime, of the legend that there had been a female English Pope (*Flowers Scattered on the Grave of Pope Joan*), and an edition, in 1696, of Johann Burchard's scurrilous diary of life at the court of the Borgia Pope Alexander VI (the only one of Leibniz's works to get onto the Vatican's *Index of Prohibited Books*). But despite a permanently agonised conscience, he never started on the history itself. It is ironical that his employers really wanted only a readable but authoritative little book which would impress their rivals.

Diplomat and academician (1698–1714)

Leibniz's access to different courts, together with his genealogical expertise, made him diplomatically very useful to Hanover. Already in 1676 he had published a lengthy treatise, which rapidly went through five editions, defending the right of German states to be treated as sovereign, and not merely as vassals of the Emperor. For this he adopted the fanciful pseudonym *Caesarinus Fürstenerius*, or 'Prince-as-Emperor'. Later, he managed to persuade Anton Ulrich of Brunswick to drop his claim to the ninth Electorate of the German Empire, and in 1692 it was Ernst August who was duly elevated to the status of Elector of Hanover. Ernst August died in 1698, and under his successor, the Elector Georg Ludwig, intra-dynastic relations became strained almost to the point of war. The main bone of contention was whether France should be contained by a strong federation of northern states (the Hanoverian policy) or by appeasement. In 1702, just before the outbreak of the War of the Spanish Succession, Leibniz was summoned home from Brunswick after failing to persuade Anton Ulrich to break his alliance with France; but his personal ties remained as strong as ever, and he soon resumed his commuting.

For many years Leibniz busied himself with the question of the English succession, especially in his role as confidant to Sophie, Ernst August's wife. The 1689 Bill of Rights, by excluding Catholics from the throne of England, made it almost inevitable that the succession would pass through Elizabeth of Bohemia (James I's daughter, and Sophie's mother), and hence to Sophie's eldest son, Georg Ludwig. The presumption was eventually enshrined in the Act of Succession of 1701; but both before and after the passing of the act, there were delicate negotiations between London and Hanover. Leibniz later prided himself on the importance of his role in these discussions; but in fact he had no official status, and may even have endangered matters by his naïve intriguing with the Scottish spy, Ker of Kersland. Most of his published writings in his last few years were pamphlets about British politics (for example, his *Anti-Jacobite* of 1715).

Evidently, Leibniz saw himself as an authority on questions of succession, since he wrote memoranda and pamphlets on every important case (in particular the Spanish and Austrian successions after the death of Charles II of Spain in 1700, and the Tuscan succession in 1713). In 1700 he was invited by Georg Ludwig's sister, the Electress Sophie Charlotte of Brandenburg to help in negotiations to have her husband Friedrich elevated to the status of King of Prussia, but he received her letter just too late to take part. The following year he was twice in Berlin promoting Hanoverian policy against the pro-French faction. In 1708 he went on a secret but inconclusive mission to Vienna on behalf of the Duke of Brunswick, and against the interests of Hanover, in order to obtain part of the Bishopric of Hildesheim for the House of

Brunswick. The Duke of Hanover was furious that Leibniz had gone away for four months without permission, but he never found out what he had actually been involved in. A few months later, Leibniz suggested to the Duke of Brunswick that he take him into his full-time service, but nothing came of this. Over the next few years, he was still carrying out minor diplomatic tasks for Hanover in Vienna.

Of all Leibniz's enthusiasms around the turn of the century, the dominant one was the promotion of scientific academies. He was involved in tentative schemes for Mainz, Hanover, Hamburg and Poland; but his main efforts were devoted to specific proposals for Berlin, Dresden, Vienna and St Petersburg. He had been lobbying for an academy in Berlin since 1695, using the good offices of the Electress Sophie Charlotte, with whom he was on very close terms. He first went to Berlin in person during 1698, and on a subsequent visit in 1700 the Elector Friedrich gave final approval to the project, and also to proposals, less fully worked out, for an observatory and a Book Commission. Leibniz himself was made Life President of the 'Brandenburg Society of the Sciences', and given a Brandenburg Court Councillorship, with an expense account of 600 thalers a year to cover the costs of an annual tour of duty in Berlin. This, incidentally, was the first occasion on which his name was given as 'von' Leibniz, although nothing is known about any official elevation to the barony. The society was not in itself particularly successful. Although it met regularly to discuss scientific papers, only one volume of its proceedings was ever published, and Leibniz was generally disappointed with the standard of the papers (apart from the many he wrote himself). However, it did add to the growing prestige of Prussia, and it formed the basis of the later *Deutsche Akademie der Wissenschaften zu Berlin.*

After his initial success in Prussia, Leibniz made considerable efforts during 1703–4 to persuade the Elector of Saxony to set up a similar institution in Dresden, but nothing came of the project. A few years later he was much more nearly successful in Vienna, where early in 1712 the Emperor made him an Imperial Councillor and appointed him Director of the proposed academy. However, it did not finally come into existence until after Leibniz's death. Lastly, in the period between 1711 and 1716, he managed to obtain frequent audiences with Peter the Great of Russia on three different trips to Europe. He persuaded him of the value of a scientific academy for St Petersburg, but again his efforts did not bear fruit until after his death. However, he was once more (in 1712) rewarded with a salaried court appointment as adviser on mathematics and science. The Tsar was very keen to foster scientific co-operation between Russia and Europe, and promised to commission research on the position of magnetic north (which would assist a project of Leibniz's for a magnetic globe as a navigational aid); on whether there was a land bridge between Russia and America; and on the origins of the Slavs and their language, for which Leibniz wrote a preliminary essay.

Besides promoting scientific societies, Leibniz never lost any opportunity to advocate other pet schemes. One in particular was his idea that the German economy might be rejuvenated by introducing silk production. He himself experimented on it in his own garden, using mulberry trees grown from seeds imported from Italy. In 1703 he was granted production licences in both Berlin and Dresden, and in the former city the industry became quite important later in the century. Other projects he suggested for Berlin included a public health system, a fire service, a land drainage scheme, and steam-powered fountains; and he was also asked for his advice on the design of a new palace and gardens. For Vienna he proposed street lighting, a state bank, an isolation hospital for plague victims, improvements in cartography and surveying, a river management scheme for the Danube, control of the corn trade, and the setting up of linen production.

After becoming involved with Berlin and Vienna, Leibniz spent less time at home than away. By 1712 he was in the pay of five different courts: Hanover, Brunswick-Lüneburg, Berlin, Vienna and St Petersburg (Celle had by now been amalgamated with Hanover). Not surprisingly, he was constantly receiving complaints from all of them about his not giving value for money, and periodically had one or other salary stopped until he reappeared. The strongest complaints came from Hanover, where Georg Ludwig not unreasonably thought that he had first claim on Leibniz's services – and the history of the Guelf family had now been in preparation for over thirty years. In the autumn of 1712, Leibniz went back to Vienna and tried unsuccessfully to get a full-time post (open to non-Catholics) as Chancellor of the Siebenburgen. He stayed there for nearly two years, ignoring repeated commands to return to Hanover. Nor was he moved by rumours that he had become a Catholic spy, the stopping of his Hanover salary, or the death of his patroness the Electress Sophie. He finally came back in September 1714, on hearing of the death of Queen Anne and of Georg Ludwig's accession to the English throne. On arrival, he discovered that Georg Ludwig had left for England three days earlier.

Last years (1714–16)

The usual picture of Leibniz's last years is one of miserable neglect in Hanover. It is true that he was rather miserable, but not because he particularly wanted to be in England. Still less had he suddenly acquired a yearning to emigrate with the court he had been doing his best to avoid for forty years. The only member of the court still alive with whom he was on really good terms was Georg Ludwig himself. Georg had consistently protected Leibniz from the hostility of the Court Council, he had been remarkably tolerant of his many foibles, and he even took him on holiday when he visited Hanover in the summer of 1716.

Leibniz's problem was that he was now in his late sixties and getting too infirm either to travel around as he used to, or to start a new life elsewhere. He did propose going to London, and in 1715 he made the extraordinary suggestion that he should be made the official historian of England. But he was much more tempted by Paris. Despite his anti-French politics, he had been invited there by Louis XIV, and would probably have gone if Louis had not died in 1715. At the same time he was actively considering a move to Vienna, and he even started negotiations to buy some property there. Other possibilities were Berlin, where he was still president of the Academy, and St Petersburg, where he held a councillorship.

He had the unwritten history of the Guelfs very much on his conscience, and worked extremely hard at it. He still hoped not merely that he would finish it before he died, but that having finished it he would then have time to get down to some serious philosophical writing. As it happens, some of his most important philosophical correspondence dates from this period (for example with the English theologian, Samuel Clarke, and with the French Jesuit, Bartholomew des Bosses). But the history and the philosophical *magnum opus* were not to be.

On 14 November 1716, after a week in bed with gout and colic, Leibniz died peacefully in the presence of his amanuensis and his coachman. He was seventy years old. The rump of the Council still in Hanover refused to attend his funeral, but he was buried with otherwise proper ceremony in the Neustädter Kirche.

Character sketch

Leibniz's life was dominated by an unachievable ambition to excel in every sphere of intellectual and political activity. The wonder is not that he failed so often, but that he achieved as much as he did. His successes were due to a rare combination of sheer hard work, a receptivity to the ideas of others, and supreme confidence in the fertility of his own mind. Whenever he tackled a new subject, he would read everything he could lay his hands on, but without submitting to orthodox concepts and assumptions. On the other hand, his desire to produce monuments to his genius, which would be both complete and all his own work, made it impossible for him to finish anything. Despite all his notes, letters and articles, he never wrote a systematic treatise on any of his special interests. His assistant Eckhart put it nicely when he said of the Guelf project that, as with numbers, Leibniz knew how to extend his historical journey to infinity.

His self-importance led him into spending too much time travelling from one court to another, and ingratiating himself with the aristocracy. When he was younger he had a reputation as an elegant courtier, *savant*, and wit (the Duchess of Orléans said of him: 'It's so rare for intellectuals to be smartly dressed, and not to smell, and to understand jokes'). But in his later years he was an object of ridicule for his old-fashioned and over-ornate clothes, his enormous black wig and his half-baked schemes. Georg Ludwig's younger brother once described him as an 'archaeological find', and suggested that Peter the Great must have taken him for the Duke of Wolfenbüttel's clown.

There were all sorts of reasons why he should have been

resented by his fellow councillors. He started off as a Frenchified outsider from Leipzig; he was exempted from normal humdrum duties; he spent most of his time travelling abroad and socialising far above his station (in particular with female royalty, such as Queen Sophie Charlotte of Prussia, and the Electress Sophie of Hanover); he interfered in the business of his colleagues, but never did the job he was being paid for; and he managed to gross an exceptionally high salary (he was obsessed with money, and kept on nagging his employers for rises and expenses). But perhaps the most serious sources of suspicion were his un-Hanoverian allegiance to rival (and sometimes hostile) states, and his hobnobbing with Papists and Jesuits. And if his colleagues suspected him of being a crypto-Catholic, the townspeople saw him as an atheist, since he never went to church. He was given the nickname *Lövenix* ('believer in nothing') – on which he commented, characteristically, that he was indeed a *believer* in nothing, since he believed only what he *knew*.

Leibniz's unpopularity at home was the inevitable price he had to pay for his universalist vision in politics and religion. He was indeed prepared to sacrifice the narrow interests of his own state and sect for a wider unity, and this set him against the nationalism and sectarianism of his age. It is sad that he spent his declining years among people who regarded him as a pampered traitor; but he would probably have fared no better as a resident alien in Paris, Vienna, Berlin or London.

2 Mathematics

The cult of the virtuoso

Throughout the seventeenth century, the majority of university mathematicians continued in the restricted tradition of scholasticism, and the main impetus for mathematical advance came from the Renaissance humanist reaction against the universities. The most fruitful and original research was carried out by gifted amateurs, who were sometimes called *virtuosi*, as being endowed with a special, individual genius (or *virtù*, in Italian). This tendency to single people out as intellectual heroes fostered a spirit of competitive individualism, rather than of co-operative research – an attitude which probably encouraged the development of new ideas, but which tended to recede as mathematics became more and more technical.

The competitive spirit gave rise to considerable jealousies as to priority over the discovery of new theorems and methods. One manifestation of this was the custom of setting challenge problems. Often the challenger had already solved the problem himself, and wanted to publicise his individual achievement. Leibniz was involved in many such challenges, and they stimulated him to a number of useful discoveries, such as equations for the curves known as the *catenary*, the *brachistochrone* and the *isochronous* curve.

The emphasis on inventive genius encouraged greater interest in ideas themselves than in their detailed elaboration. This reinforced Leibniz's natural reluctance to follow his ideas through, and to censor the wilder ones. The resultant mass of partly-formed thoughts meant that some of his best inspirations went completely unnoticed. A good example is his discovery of the basic principles of topology, for which he coined the Latin name, still sometimes used, of *analysis situs*. Leibniz saw it as complementing the analytic geometry of Descartes, which abstracts the quantitative aspect from geometrical figures drawn in space, and reduces them to purely algebraic terms. Leibniz's *analysis situs* abstracts in its turn from all quantitative features (lengths, angles, degrees of curvature, and so on), and deals only with such relationships as are left. In effect this means the study of what remains true of infinitely pliable figures, however much they may have been stretched, compressed, or otherwise deformed. Leibniz's idea remained dormant until the nineteenth century, but since then it has become central to modern mathematics – in particular for the development of non-Euclidean geometries.

Binary arithmetic

Most of Leibniz's mathematical discoveries came to him during his stay in Paris. Potentially one of the most important was that of binary arithmetic – though he was not actually the first to discover it, since it had already been thought of by Thomas Hariot early in the century, and again by Juan Caramuel y Lobkowitz in 1670. Leibniz himself later came to believe that the Chinese must have known about it, on the grounds that it was implicit in the theory of i ching.

The binary system is the simplest possible notation for numerals. Our ordinary decimal system has a choice of ten characters for each place (units, tens, hundreds, etc.). In the binary system there are only two characters: one to designate an empty place, the other to mark that it is filled. If the places can be defined independently, for example by a grid, all that is needed is an arbitrary mark or signal wherever a place is filled. Using the convention of 0 for empty, and 1 for filled, the system runs as follows:

0	1	2	3	4	5	6	7	8	9	etc.
0	1	10	11	100	101	110	111	1000	1001	etc.

Although Leibniz was tremendously proud of his discovery, he did very little with it. Unlike Lobkowitz and modern mathematicians, he failed to generalise it into a theory of modular arithmetic with its own special theorems. Nor, apart from one very tentative draft, did he try to design a calculating machine which used it. It may seem odd to us, in the age of the computer, that someone who invented both a calculator and binary arithmetic should not have put the two together, and come up with something closer in principle to the modern computer. But in the context of the technology of the time, a binary machine would only have increased Leibniz's difficulties. There would have been more wheels, more friction, more carrying, and there would have had to be an extra mechanism for translating between binary and decimal, in order to make the calculator usable by ordinary people. The binary system came into its own only with the advent of electronics. As far as Leibniz was concerned, the greatest significance of his discovery was metaphysical, or indeed mystical, as showing how the whole universe could be seen as constructed out of Number. We shall come back to this in Chapter 6.

The infinitesimal calculus

By far the most important of Leibniz's mathematical achievements was his discovery of the infinitesimal calculus, which he made at the end of his Paris period, in 1675. As before, he was not the first – Newton beat him to it by nine years – though Leibniz was the first to publish the discovery, in 1684.

The significance of the calculus is so great that it is

generally held to mark the starting-point of modern mathematics. Moreover, any development of physics beyond the point reached by Newton would have been virtually impossible without the calculus. In general terms, what it does is to make curves and variable quantities amenable to the sort of mathematical treatment which had previously been exclusive to constants, straight lines, and certain curves easily constructible from straight lines (circles, and conic sections, or curves obtained by slicing cones at various angles). Since almost all physical quantities are in a state of regular variation, a general technique for subjecting these variations to mathematical analysis is a prerequisite of any adequate physical science.

The infinitesimal calculus has two parts: the differential and the integral calculus. The differential calculus provides a general method for determining the rate of change at any instant of a quantity which is continuously changing in relation to another quantity of which it is a 'function'. Leibniz was, incidentally, the first person to use the word 'function' in this modern sense of a variable, the value of which is uniquely determined by some other variable (as, for example, the distance covered by a falling body is a 'function' of the time it has been falling). Applications of the differential calculus include the calculation of planetary orbits; describing the motion of pendulums, waves or vibrating strings; finding values of otherwise insoluble equations; establishing highest and lowest values of functions; calculating the bending of loaded beams – and so on.

Integration is the reverse of differentiation, and consists in reconstructing a whole from a given value at an instant – in other words, in going up one dimension. From a rate of change at a point you can reconstruct a whole line, from a line you can reconstruct an area it defines, and from an area you can specify the volume created by rotating it. The technique is essential for determining centres of gravity, moments of inertia of rotating bodies such as fly-wheels, and other more complicated applications. However, its scope is somewhat more limited than that of differentiation, since information is lost in moving down one dimension through differentiation, and a whole cannot always be unambiguously reconstructed. Leibniz failed to appreciate this limitation – a mistake which influenced his metaphysics by reinforcing his belief that absolutely *any* whole could in principle be regenerated from *any* of its parts.

Leibniz was much exercised by the problem of the logical respectability of infinitesimal quantities. At the time, mathematicians generally insisted that the objects of mathematics should be *real*, in the sense of being representable geometrically. They were deeply suspicious of 'imaginary' quantities which could not be constructed by ruler and compass – for instance, $\sqrt{-1}$. Infinitesimals, such as rates of change at an instant, clearly fell into this class. For example, speed is change of distance divided by time; but at an *instant*, no time elapses and no distance is travelled – so the notion of distance divided by time is strictly meaningless. As Leibniz wrote to Bartholomew des Bosses in 1706:

Infinitesimals are mental fictions, though they have their place in calculations, like imaginary roots in algebra. (G ii 305)

Although Leibniz went along with the prejudice that infinitesimals needed a geometrical foundation, the route by which he arrived at the calculus was algebraic rather than geometrical. His discovery arose from the concept of an infinite series converging on a limit: the differential calculus was a technique for determining the *limit* of such a series, and the integral calculus for finding its *sum*.

Leibniz's earlier researches in Paris had been directed in particular towards the age-old problem of squaring the circle. Traditionally, the problem was that of finding a method for constructing a square of exactly the same area as a given circle. In algebraic terms, it meant giving an exact numerical value to π (pi), that is, to the ratio between the circumference and the diameter of a circle. Closer and closer approximations had been obtained by taking regular polygons with more and more sides fitting just outside and just inside a circle, and calculating the difference between the lengths of their circumferences. But these results were necessarily only approximate.

Leibniz believed that he had made an important step towards the goal of a precise value for π, when he discovered for himself an infinite series of which the sum would be exactly $\dfrac{\pi}{4}$.

This series went as follows: $\dfrac{1}{1} - \dfrac{1}{3} + \dfrac{1}{5} - \dfrac{1}{7} + \quad \cdots$

All that was needed was a method for calculating the sum of the series. It was eventually recognised that this was an impossibility. Given the diameter of a circle, any numerical expression for the length of its circumference would run to infinite decimal places. But, spurred on by his partial success, Leibniz worked intensively at the theory of infinite series and their summation. In the course of his labours, he produced a number of results of considerable importance in their own right. To give just one example, he discovered what has since become known as 'Leibniz's test' for whether an infinite series will converge on a single limit.

Of course he never found his crock of gold of squaring the circle, but his researches did lead up to the far greater prize of the infinitesimal calculus. What he discovered was that the gradient of a curve at a point (corresponding to a rate of change at an instant) could be treated as the limiting value of an infinite series generated by the gradients of shorter and shorter straight lines. It was from this that he developed the process of differentiation as a general technique. Similarly, the area under a curve could be treated as the sum of an infinite series generated by the varying lengths of infinitely many, infinitely thin strips under the curve. It was the generalisation of this process which led to the technique of integration.

Leibniz's work on the calculus was, if anything, more successful even than he realised. If he had fulfilled his ambition of squaring the circle, his discovery would have been self-contained, whereas the discovery of the calculus ushered in a whole new era of mathematics. As for his failure to give a sound geometrical basis to the calculus, it was precisely the fact that he approached the issue algebraically that made his system superior to Newton's.

The priority dispute

While Leibniz was developing and publicising his calculus during the last decades of the century, he remained genuinely unaware that Newton had discovered it before him. During his Paris period, he learned from a brief correspondence with Newton that the latter had made certain advances in the direction of the calculus, but Newton's letters revealed nothing about his general method. Leibniz's impression must have been confirmed much later, in 1689, on his first reading of Newton's *Principles of Mathematical Philosophy*, since the work was presented almost entirely in terms of traditional mathematics. This was despite the fact that the calculus was indispensable for some of the proofs, and would have made most of the rest far less cumbersome and obscure.

Leibniz knew that the calculus was of tremendous importance, and he could not believe that his rival would have deliberately suppressed it just where it would have been most useful. In this he was adopting a characteristically futurist perspective, seeing his own work and that of his contemporaries in the light of future advances yet unmade. We too tend to see the *Principles* historically, as inaugurating the 'Age of Newton', and so we can easily share Leibniz's puzzlement at the omission of the calculus. By contrast, Newton himself believed he was fulfulling the prophetic work of his ancient and modern predecessors, rather than creating something entirely new. He was therefore more motivated to stress his continuity with the giants on whose shoulders he was standing. Quite apart from this, there was the purely practical consideration that he could expect a much wider readership for a work that presupposed only conventional mathematics.

Even when Newton's 'method of fluxions' was eventually unveiled in print, it was by no means obvious that it was essentially the same as Leibniz's infinitesimal calculus. His approach was basically geometrical; his terminology was suspiciously reminiscent of the scholastic jargon of the 'flowing' of points and lines; and his notation, which involved the addition or subtraction of dots over letters, was clumsy and difficult to work with. Leibniz's approach, on the other hand, was algebraical; his language was fresh and appropriate, incorporating such terms as *differential*, *integral*, *coordinate* and *function*; and his notation, which we still use today, was clear and elegant. It was based on the letter *d* for 'difference' (as in $\frac{dy}{dx}$, the symbol for a differential), and the contemporary long *s* (∫) for 'sum', or integral.

If matters had rested with Newton and Leibniz, there

would probably have been no particular quarrel between them. But early in the 1700s, their supporters on opposite sides of the Channel started squabbling about the respective merits of the two systems, and about the priority of their discovery. Newton and Leibniz were soon drawn into the dispute, which became unpleasantly acrimonious. In particular, Leibniz had to defend himself against charges of plagiarising Newton's letters during the early seventies, and of subsequently tampering with the evidence.

It is beyond reasonable doubt that Leibniz's discovery was in fact independent, but the nationalistic fervour aroused by the dispute, and the incontrovertible evidence in favour of Newton's priority, had disastrous consequences for English mathematics. While the Continental mathematicians of the eighteenth century made great strides in the theory of the calculus, and in its applications to Newtonian physics, the English stuck loyally to Newton's own much less suitable method of fluxions, and remained in a backwater for over a century.

3 Science

Force and energy

Leibniz's major contribution to science lay in his clarification
of certain key concepts in dynamics. Theorists were still
struggling to turn the vague notions of everyday life into
precise scientific concepts. The first step, due primarily to
Galileo, had been to abandon the common-sense assumption
that things stop moving unless they are kept going by a force,
and to postulate instead the principle that things *conserve* their
motion *unless* acted upon by a force. Descartes tried to
systematise the laws of motion Galileo had established, but he
ran into difficulties because of ambiguities in expressions like
'quantity of motion' and 'force'. Leibniz's earliest success,
acting on suggestions he owed to Huygens in Paris, was to
give a clear diagnosis of the deficiencies in Descartes' conceptual apparatus.

Descartes based his system on a law of the conservation of
motion. His idea was that God, having created the world of
matter, then set it in motion; and although motions could be
exchanged between one thing and another, and the direction
in which things moved could change, the total quantity
of motion had to remain constant. Leibniz showed that
Descartes' formulation was seriously confused in at least two
respects.

The first confusion was that Descartes talked of *motion*,
without making an adequate distinction between *speed* and
velocity. Speed is a measure of distance covered in a particular
time, whereas velocity is what is known as a *vector* quantity,
and is a measure of distance covered *in a particular direction* in

a particular time. Leibniz saw that if anything was conserved it had to be velocity rather than speed, otherwise changes in the directions in which things moved would not be subject to any conservation law.

Descartes himself was well aware of this loophole in his mechanics, and actually exploited it in order to account for the influence of mind over matter. He believed that human behaviour was controlled by the direction of motion of tiny particles in the cavities of the brain, which made them enter this nerve rather than that. The principal seat of the soul was the pineal gland, situated in the main cavity at the centre of the brain. The soul could use the gland to deflect the direction of motion of particles without itself adding any new motion, rather as the rider of a horse can change its direction without actually *pushing* it round himself. But, as Leibniz pointed out, the soul would have to exert some sort of physical force in order to move the pineal gland so as to change the direction of motion of particles in the brain – and how an immaterial soul could influence matter was precisely what needed explaining in the first place.

The second problem with Descartes' concept of quantity of motion was its inability to relate a fast motion of a small body to a slow motion of a large one. Here again metaphysical considerations were involved. Descartes wanted to base his account of reality on the simplest possible metaphysical categories, and opted for the directly measurable, spatio-temporal properties of size, shape and motion, as constituting the essence of the material world. That is, he saw the physical universe as consisting of nothing but sizes, shapes and relative positions changing through time. In Descartes' terminology, the essence of matter was geometrical *extension*. However, Leibniz showed that the dynamically relevant measure of an object's size was not its geometrical dimensions, but its *mass*.

So, instead of talking loosely of 'size' times 'motion' as being conserved, Descartes should have defined 'quantity of motion' as *mass* times *velocity* – in other words, as *momentum*.

As it happens, momentum *is* conserved in certain systems – for example, hard balls colliding on a plane surface (as in snooker). But Leibniz showed that in the case of *falling* bodies, it is not momentum, but a different measure of energy that is conserved. He explained the distinction by means of the following thought-experiment. A certain weight falling through a certain distance will obviously release the same amount of energy as something four times the weight falling through a quarter of the distance. But the velocity of a falling body is proportional only to the square root of the distance travelled, so that the momentum of the smaller weight will only be a multiple of $1 \times \sqrt{4} = 2$, whereas that of the larger weight will be a multiple of $4 \times \sqrt{1} = 4$. Leibniz concluded that, to compensate for the effect of the square root, there had to be a quantity proportional to the mass (m) times the *square* of the velocity (v), which would be the true measure of the energy conserved in all interactions. He called this quantity *vis viva* ('live force/energy/power' – the concepts were not yet distinguished), and he assumed that it was simply mv^2. In this he came very close to the modern concept of *kinetic energy*, or $\frac{1}{2}mv^2$, which a body has by virtue of its motion.

There are, however, considerable problems over the extent to which kinetic energy is conserved. For a start, there needs to be a complementary *potential* energy, which a body has by virtue of its position. Thus, if the energy of a swinging pendulum is to be constant, it will all be in the form of kinetic energy at the bottom of the swing, and of potential energy at the top. Leibniz did postulate what he called 'dead force' (*vis mortua*), but he made this a much more general concept, covering all forms of force that were not manifest in actual motion (centrifugal force, for instance).

A more serious problem is that our everyday experience includes innumerable instances of kinetic energy being generated out of completely different forms of energy, and the other way round – for example, an animal waking up, gunpowder exploding, steam pushing out of a boiling kettle, brakes stopping a moving vehicle. Leibniz's explanation of the dissipation of kinetic energy through friction is plausible enough: the energy is taken up by faster motions of the particles of the bodies concerned – they get hotter. In the other cases, however, there is no independent evidence that the energy pre-exists in the form of motions among the particles of the muscles, gunpowder, or unburnt fuel. Instances such as these show the need for a non-mechanical concept of energy, and it is here that Leibniz's explanations become metaphysical rather than scientific. We shall look at the metaphysical dimension of Leibniz's theory of energy in greater detail in Chapter 5.

Dynamics and kinematics

As significant as his critique of Descartes' mechanics was Leibniz's attack on Newton's account of force. In the *Principles*, Newton limited himself to describing interactions between bodies in terms of general mathematical laws. This limitation was both a strength and a weakness. Newton succeeded in making the complexities of nature amenable to mathematical description only by simplifying the phenomena: by treating material particles as if they were infinitely hard yet infinitely elastic, concentrated at points, capable of exchanging any amount of force all at once, connected by forces operating instantaneously at a distance, and so on.

Leibniz complained that this made Newton's system an

idealised abstraction, which could not possibly be true of the real world. In reality, nothing was absolutely hard or elastic, nothing happened instantaneously, and every causal interaction was mediated by a complex mechanism. In general terms, Newton would have agreed with Leibniz's comment. He too believed in underlying mechanisms, but he refused to speculate about them in the *Principles* (his famous, 'I do not invent hypotheses').

A more damaging criticism which Leibniz brought against Newton was that he gave pseudo-explanations in terms of magical 'occult virtues'. Just as Molière had joked about the scholastic explanation that opium sends one to sleep because of its 'dormitive virtue', so Leibniz laughed at Newton for explaining the *gravity* of things as due to a *gravitational* force. The trouble was that Newton's forces were defined in terms of directly measurable masses and changes in velocity. This meant that these masses and velocities themselves were the primary realities. The forces he postulated added nothing new to reality, and therefore explained nothing.

Leibniz held that it was not enough to formulate mechanical laws to describe and predict the behaviour of physical systems. A genuine science also had to *explain* the phenomena by postulating underlying mechanisms and powers of which perceptible motions were the results. Motions must be derived from powers, not powers from motions. In other words, what was needed was a *dynamics*, or science of powers, not just a *kinematics*, or science of motions. This requirement dominated Leibniz's approach to two scientific questions which were to have a significant influence on his metaphysics: gravitation, and the transfer of forces between colliding bodies.

In the *New Physical Hypothesis*, which comprised the two treatises dedicated to the Royal Society and the Paris Academy in 1671, Leibniz outlined a comprehensive account of all forms of motion to be found in the universe. He started with an abstract theory of the laws of motion in general, and then proceeded to suggest mechanisms for various particular phenomena, such as planetary motion, certain chemical reactions, and the cohesion of solids. His explanation of planetary motion, which derived ultimately from Descartes, was intended to show how the sun could force the planets to travel in their orbits simply by means of *pushing*. He suggested that space was filled with an ether of extremely fine particles, and that a rotation of the sun set up circular motions ('vortices') in the ether, which pushed the planets round like boats in a whirlpool. His theory was, of course, wrong, but at least it took full account of the need to explain the transference of mechanical forces from one body to another in a finite time, in contrast with Newton's gravitational force, which was supposed to operate instantaneously, over a distance, and by simple attraction.

Much later, in his *Specimen of Dynamics* (1695), Leibniz tried to give an account of the mechanism which mediated exchanges of force between colliding bodies. In real collisions (unlike Newton's idealisations), there had to be a finite period during which one body slowed down and the other picked up speed. This implied that bodies had a certain size, and were not absolutely hard or elastic, since the only conceivable mechanism for transfer of force was that bodies were first squashed together, and then gradually sprang back from each other once all the kinetic energy had been taken up. However, as soon as it is accepted that transfer of force between everyday objects must be mediated by a mechanism, there is no point at which you stop needing smaller and smaller sub-mechanisms. At no level can you suddenly say that force is transferred *directly*.

Elasticity is itself a phenomenon requiring explanation in terms of pushings of particles. At the first instant of impact, the outermost particles of each colliding body push against their neighbours, and these in turn push against *their* neighbours, and so on right through each body. But then each of *these* pushings needs to be explained by the compression of sub-particles, and so on to infinity. The conclusion Leibniz drew was that, ultimately, forces were not really transferred at all. All action was, as he put it, *spontaneous*. The energy required for a body's motion on the occasion of an impact, had to be drawn from its own resources, since it could not actually take up any energy from bodies impinging on it.

Leibniz's theory of the spontaneity of all motion is not as silly as it might seem. It is a commonplace that every force has an equal and opposite reaction. In the case of colliding bodies, the reaction is the force holding each body together. If either of the bodies has less cohesive force than the kinetic energy involved in the collision, it will shatter instead of moving as predicted by the laws of mechanics. So Leibniz was right to say that bodies can take up only as much energy as they have the capacity to absorb, even though it does not follow that they cannot absorb energy from each other at all.

An even more significant aspect of the theory was its abandonment of the traditional notion that matter was essentially inert. Leibniz saw that if the only function of matter was as a passive carrier of forces, then it had no role to play in scientific explanation. Its only role would be the metaphysical one of satisfying the prejudice that forces must inhere in something more substantial than themselves. He maintained that matter was nothing other than the receptive capacity of things, or their 'passive power', as he called it. Matter just *was* the capacity to slow other things down, and to be accelerated rather than penetrated (capacities which ghosts and shadows lack) – in other words, inertia or mass, and solidity. So, taking also into account 'active powers' such as kinetic energy, Leibniz reduced matter to a complex of forces. In this he was anticipating modern field theory, which treats material particles as concentrated fields of force – an anticipation duly recognised by its founder, the Italian mathematician Ruggiero Giuseppe Boscovich (1711–87).

However, although Leibniz was ahead of his time in aiming at a genuine dynamics, it was this very ambition that prevented him from matching the achievement of his rival Newton. Newton succeeded in producing a comprehensive theory of kinematics precisely because he avoided 'inventing hypotheses' about dynamics, or the powers and mechanisms underlying the kinematics. It was only by simplifying the issues in this way, that Newton succeeded in reducing them to manageable proportions.

Entropy

Leibniz's perception of his own scientific and philosophical position was, to an important extent, defined by reference to his interpretation of Newton. It is therefore surprising that there was no direct confrontation between the two men in later life. The nearest was an exchange of letters between Leibniz and Newton's friend, the theologian Samuel Clarke, who wrote in close consultation with Newton himself. In a letter of November 1715 to Caroline, Princess of Wales, Leibniz had criticised certain theological implications of Newton's physics, and she had invited Clarke to reply. In accordance with custom, both sides wrote with a view to eventual publication, and the letters were in fact printed in 1717, within a year of Leibniz's death. The two most important topics of the correspondence were entropy, and whether space was absolute or relative.

At the very end of the *Optics*, Newton had suggested that God might eventually have to intervene in order to restore the orderly motions of the planets. Leibniz read this as implying that the clockwork of nature would eventually run down unless God wound it up from time to time. In other words, God would prevent a state of entropy, in which all energy would have become evenly distributed, and therefore incapable of doing any work. At one level, the argument was overtly theological: Leibniz claimed that it was blasphemy to suppose that God would need to correct what he had created; Clarke replied that it was tantamount to atheism to suppose that creation could function without God. But at another level, they were really having a scientific argument about the conservation of energy.

Leibniz assumed as a basic principle of the mechanistic world-view, that the total amount of energy in the universe remains constant. That there can be no *increase* in energy, is equivalent to saying that there can be no interference from outside – no Cartesian deflections of particles in the brain by the immaterial soul, no Newtonian adjustments to planetary orbits by God. God might miraculously suspend the laws of nature as part of his divine plan, but it makes no sense to suppose that the ordinary workings of nature might depend on miraculous interventions.

That there can be no *decrease* in the amount of energy, Leibniz took as implying that the universe as a whole must be a perpetual motion. Although he strenuously denied that there could be perpetual motion machines *within* the universe, he was wrong about the universe as a whole, since he failed to take account of the fact that work is only achieved in a system in which energy passes from a part with a higher level of energy to one with a lower level. So, the more work that is done in the universe, the more evenly energy is spread, and the less capacity for further work remains. The universe will indeed eventually run down.

Part of the reason for Leibniz's mistake was the limitation of his concept of energy to *kinetic* energy, which cannot exist without motion. He believed that whenever a mechanism ran down through friction, the energy would always be taken up by motions of particles, with the consequence that motion in the universe could never cease. But even with this conception of energy, Leibniz failed to see that the law of the conservation of energy would still permit the universe to degenerate into a gas of randomly moving particles with the same total kinetic energy as at present.

In fact, what is lost as the universe approaches a state of entropy is not energy, but what is now known as *information*, or the degree to which it is non-random: variety and order give way to uniformity and chaos. So what Leibniz really needed in order to deny that the universe would naturally run down, was a 'principle of the conservation of information'. As it happens, he did believe in such a principle, but his reasons for it were metaphysical rather than scientific.

The relativity of space

The other main point at issue in the correspondence with Clarke was the question of whether space was absolute or relative. Newton's system was premised on the assumption that there was an absolute difference between a body's being at rest, in motion, or under acceleration. The distinction required the concept of a fixed frame of reference, such as the 'fixed stars', to define the absolute space relative to which bodies moved or accelerated. As for what space *was*, over and above the bodies in it, Newton proposed in the *Optics* an analogy with the 'sensorium', or subjective perceptual space. We mortals perceived things by means of perceptual images in our private sensoria, whereas God perceived things them-selves directly, and the real space they occupied was nothing other than God's sensorium.

Leibniz opened with objections to Newton's theology, but he soon progressed to a fundamental critique of the very notion of absolute space. His main point was that, if space was distinct from everything in it, then it must itself be completely uniform and homogeneous. But in that case, it could not conceivably fulfil its function as an absolute frame of *reference*, since it would have no markers to which one could refer, in order to tell whether anything moved relative to it. We could *imagine* lines, like the grid lines on a map, relative to which we might suppose things to be moving. But there were no such lines marked out in real space, and even if there were, we could have no grounds for saying *they* were stationary. Conse-quently, it made no sense to suppose some privileged frame of reference as absolutely at rest, whether the fixed stars, or real space itself.

Leibniz's conclusion was that space was unreal. He thought it was a mere superstition to suppose that there was some imperceptible container which the whole of the material universe was 'in'. Ultimately, only *things* existed. We could make true statements about their 'order of coexistence' – statements like 'Mercury is nearer the Sun than Venus' – but space itself was an abstraction. The only basis for truths about spatial relations was how they appeared to different observers, especially to God as the only unbiased and perspective-free observer.

Given Leibniz's relativism about space, it is natural to ask how far he anticipated Einstein's theory of relativity. This is not an easy question to answer, since Leibniz, unlike Einstein, did not produce any mathematical theory of his own to rival Newton's. But the very fact that he failed to attempt an alternative theory suggests that his difference was metaphysical rather than scientific. Leibniz's main concern was not with Newton's mathematical formulae as such, but with his belief in the independent reality of space. If Leibniz could have been confronted with Einstein's theory, at least as popularly expounded, he might well have wanted to make the same points against it as he had made against Newton's. The main difference between an Einsteinian and a Newtonian account of space is that the former gives it a complex structure, as contrasted with the homogeneity of Newtonian space. Leibniz's position was that space was not a *thing* capable of having any structure at all, whether simple or complex. So, philosophically he was more radically relativist than Einstein, even though he had nothing to set against Newton as a scientist.

4 Logic

The role of logic

Leibniz was exceptional among his contemporaries for his belief in the importance of logic. This is undoubtedly a major reason for the recent revival of interest in Leibniz's philosophy, now that logic has regained a central position on the philosophical stage, for the first time since the heyday of scholasticism.

Ever since the ancient Greeks first tried to systematise the principles of good reasoning, logic was in constant rivalry with the art of rhetoric. Rhetoricians specialised in the refinement of concepts through the proper use of language. Logicians, on the other hand, aimed to abstract completely from the subject matter or *content* of reasoning, and deal exclusively with purely *formal* relationships among concepts, and among propositions composed out of concepts. Just as mathematicians used letters such as x and y to stand for any number, so logicians learned to do the same for concepts. Until Leibniz, however, little was done to avoid the imprecisions of ordinary language by symbolical representation of the logical relationships themselves.

Throughout later antiquity and the middle ages, and even into the eighteenth century in places, the standard curriculum at schools and universities included both logic and rhetoric. With the rise of scholasticism in the thirteenth and fourteenth centuries, the emphasis became heavily biased towards logic. As part of their reaction against university education in general, the humanist intellectuals of the Renaissance tended to espouse the cause of rhetoric as the only true art of reasoning. Nizolio (see p. 10) was typical of this approach.

At the end of the sixteenth century, logic was faced with a more serious challenge from the new scientific movement. It became increasingly evident that the new scientific methods far outclassed those of the old scholastic theorisers, and that they succeeded not merely through the amassing and organising of experimental data (as advocated by Bacon in particular), but through abstract problem-solving techniques which owed nothing either to traditional logic or to rhetoric.

The most popular alternative model for effective reasoning was the axiomatic method of Euclidean geometry, which systematically derived sets of theorems from a minimum of axioms and definitions. But the applicability of the method outside mathematics was highly problematic. In particular, it could not show how to draw general conclusions about the world from experience, nor how to discover or invent anything. Nevertheless, there was a brief fashion for presenting work 'in the geometrical style' – for example Newton's *Principles*, Spinoza's *Ethics* and Leibniz's own work on jurisprudence.

Most of the major philosophers of the period wrote extensively on the problem of the best method for reasoning out new truths, especially Descartes in France, and Bacon and Hobbes in England. Leibniz's approach was to try and reconcile the logical, rhetorical and geometrical traditions by blending their three distinct emphases (on formalism, on linguistic propriety and on mathematicisation) into the single vision of a formal language notated mathematically.

Definition

One of the more conventional aspects of Leibniz's logic was his acceptance of the traditional system of definition by *genus* and *differentia* (the 'method of division'). According to this approach, which stemmed ultimately from Plato and Aristotle, the proper method of defining classes of things was to start with a very general class (the *genus*), and divide it into two smaller, mutually exclusive classes (*species*) by means of some property which every member of the genus either did or did not have (the *differentia*).

Whole trees of branching classes could be defined in this way. One of the simplest and best-known examples was the so-called 'Tree of Porphyry', named after the third-century commentator on Aristotle's *Categories*. This started by dividing things into the material (bodies) and the immaterial; bodies into the animate (living things) and the inanimate; living things into those that had sensation (animals) and those that did not (vegetables); and animals into the rational (man) and the non-rational (brutes). The Tree of Porphyry served as a model for most subsequent systems of taxonomy, such as the modern classification of the animal kingdom based on the work of the English naturalist, John Ray (1627–1705), and the botanical classification devised by the Swedish taxonomist, Linnaeus (Carl von Linné, 1707–78).

In common with many of his contemporaries, Leibniz believed that, in principle, all concepts could be defined in terms of their position in one single hierarchy of this sort. And however unrealistic the ideal, it had important repercussions on his philosophy as a whole.

The method of division encouraged a belief that, at any stage, the concept defined must be more *complex* than the concepts used to define it. So, if the concept 'man' was a combination of the concepts 'rational' and 'animal', these components had to be *simpler* than the concept compounded from them. It seemed to follow that, ultimately, there must be certain absolutely simple, atomic concepts out of which all others were constructed, otherwise there would be an infinite regress. In particular, the very first, or 'highest' genus could not be defined as a species of any higher genus; and the various differentiae had to be either simple concepts themselves, or else reducible to simples by a process of definition. Obviously, any philosophy structured around the method of division had the problem of identifying the simple concepts, and of explaining how we could acquire them. We shall come back to Leibniz's solution at the beginning of Chapter 6.

At the other end of the scale, there was the question of where to stop the process of subdivision into species – in traditional terms, the problem of the 'lowest' species. In the example of the Tree of Prophyry, a biologist would say that Man was a lowest species, on the grounds that its members were inter-fertile. But a geneticist or ethnologist would recognise subspecies such as races, tribes and even families. From a purely logical point of view, it is possible to go on subdividing as long as there remain characteristics which at least one member of a species has, and others lack. Consequently, all the members of a logically lowest species will be absolutely identical with each other.

Aristotle, whose interests were primarily biological, saw an absolute difference between species-defining characteristics, and the mass of characteristics peculiar to individuals. He explained the difference in terms of an analogy with carpentry. Some of the characteristics of a carpenter's finished work are due to the form he imposes on his material, and these will be common to all pieces of furniture of the same type. Any remaining differences are due to the individual character of the wood of which each piece is made (Aristotle actually used ὕλη, the Greek word for 'wood', to mean material or matter, as contrasted with form or essence). Similarly, God the Creator imposed specific forms on different portions of matter when creating plants and animals of various species.

Medieval philosophers were much exercised by the question of whether there was an absolute distinction between formal and material characteristics, and whether individual things were individuals in virtue of having a unique set of qualities, or a unique piece of matter. This was the issue discussed by Leibniz in his undergraduate dissertation *On the Principle of Individuation.* There he sided with the thirteenth-century Irish or Northern British philosopher, John Duns Scotus (the original 'Dunce'), who held that each individual had its own *haecceity*, or 'thisness', which was distinct both from its qualities and its matter. However, Leibniz soon came to the view that the process of subdivision into species ended only with a complete description of an individual, so that to be an individual *was* to be a lowest species. He was therefore committed to what he called the 'Principle of the Identity of Indiscernibles' (now often known as 'Leibniz's Law'), to the effect that a lowest species could not have more than one member: if two things were distinct individuals, there had to be something that was true of the one but not of the other, thereby making them of different species.

Real and semi-mental beings

Leibniz believed that ultimately the only realities were individaul substances and their properties. Precisely what he meant by 'individual substances' will be one of the main topics of the next chapter. But as a first approximation, we can take him as meaning things like trees, sheep or people, in contrast with items that have only a secondary or dependent existence, such as collections of things, or relations. These secondary beings are dependent in at least two different ways.

Firstly, other things can exist without them, but they cannot exist without other things. For example, you can have sheep without having a flock, but you cannot have a flock without having sheep. Similarly, you can have two things, one of which may be larger than the other, but you cannot have a relationship of 'being larger than' without things of different sizes.

Secondly, collections and relations are as they are only in virtue of some sort of mental attitude. A flock of fifty sheep is not any arbitrary collection of fifty sheep, but fifty particular sheep considered by intelligent beings as forming a unit in relation to some specific function. For instance, they may have the same owner or be in the charge of the same shepherd, despite being scattered over the hillside or mingled with another flock. Again, relationships presuppose a particular set of criteria or point of view in respect of which they hold: a large thing is large only considered in relation to something smaller.

Leibniz called things like collections and relations 'semi-mental': semi-*mental* because they were mind-dependent, but only *semi*-mental, because they were based in reality, and true assertions could be made about them. This then invites the question of how such assertions can be *true*, if what they are true of is not fully real.

The most natural account of truth is to say that it consists in a correspondence between reality itself and a linguistic item, whether spoken, written or silently thought. For the correspondence to be perfect, it must apply at the structural level as well as at the level of content. So, given that the primary constituents of reality are substances and their properties, the basic linguistic structure will be the one that most closely mirrors the having of properties by substances. The appropriate structure is the one known as the *subject–predicate form*. In sentences of this form, the subject identifies a substance, and the predicate attributes a certain property to it. So, in the sentence 'Socrates is wise' the subject-term 'Socrates' identifies the individual substance Socrates, and the predicate 'is wise' ascribes the property of wisdom to him.

When we make true assertions about dependent beings, it ought to be possible to paraphrase what we say into sentences of the subject–predicate form, in which the subjects refer to genuine substances. For example, in the sentence 'The flock is grazing' the subject refers not to a substance, but to a collection of substances. But it could in principle be rewritten as a series of sentences about individual sheep.

However, relational statements are more problematic. Leibniz made various attempts at analysing them in terms of conjunctions of subject–predicate sentences. One example he discussed (C 287) was the sentence 'Paris is the lover of Helen', which asserts a relationship between two subjects, Paris and Helen. Leibniz said that it was equivalent to the two subject–predicate sentences 'Paris loves' and 'Helen is loved', together with the proviso that each was true only because the other was true. This type of paraphrase removed relations from *within* sentences and turned them into causal relations *between* sentences. So we should not expect relations to correspond to distinct components of reality, but to facts about why things are as they are. Ultimately, God made Paris a lover *because* he was making Helen loved, and Helen loved *because* he was making Paris a lover.

However, Leibniz was not particularly interested in tinkering with ordinary language as it was. He was mainly concerned with the possibility of an uncompromisingly ideal language in which every truth could be expressed without recourse to relational properties at all. If you could describe all the properties of substances, you could deduce any relational truths you liked, but they would give no new information about reality. For instance, if you knew the weights of two objects, the assertion that one was heavier than the other would add nothing. It would merely be a vaguer way of describing one particular aspect of the facts from which it was derived.

Leibniz's thesis that relations were not primary constituents of reality gave a new twist to his Principle of the Identity of Indiscernibles (see p. 53 above). It is a truism to say that if there are two distinct things, there must be something that is true of the one but not of the other, otherwise there could be no grounds for saying that there were two things at all. In everyday situations, the difference would normally be a relational one, such as spatial position. For example, I might hold two otherwise indiscernible objects in different hands, and it would be true of only one of them that it was in my right hand. But if, as Leibniz maintained, relational truths are reducible to truths about the intrinsic properties of substances, then it must follow that everything is *intrinsically* different from everything else.

This is a much more radical thesis than the original truism, and it gave Leibniz a further defence against the Newtonian theory of absolute space (see pp. 46 ff.). Clarke claimed that God had created innumerable atoms differing only in their spatial location, and that therefore space was the prior reality. Leibniz replied that since space was only relational, it had to depend on the diversity of related things, not the other way round. Clarke's argument showed not that space was absolute, but that there could not be two absolutely identical atoms.

Leibniz's thesis that only substances and their properties exist gave rise to another problem, namely 'the problem of existence'. As we have seen, a complete set of properties defines an individual substance. But not all possible substances are actualised. So what is the difference between a substance that *exists*, and one that does not? It cannot be any property, or equivalent to any set of properties, otherwise the existent substance actualised by God would be different from the possibility he had willed to create. Consequently, the notion of existence is essentially indefinable.

One solution which Leibniz studiously avoided was that of Locke. For Locke, the essential difference between a mere abstraction and an actual substance was that the concept of the latter included, as a distinct ingredient, the 'idea of substance in general'. Locke had to admit that the idea was the particularly obscure one of an 'I know not what', underlying and supporting its properties. Leibniz could no more define existence than Locke could, but at least he did not add to the difficulty by attributing it to an occult base, which was, as it were, garnished with properties.

In Leibniz's view, substances were nothing other than groups of existent properties. For a property to belong to, or 'inhere in' a substance was simply for it to be a member of a particular group. When people join together to form a club, there is no extra entity over and above the membership (some 'club-in-itself') to which every member directly belongs. Similarly with existent things, there is no extra entity (an underlying substance, or 'thing-in-itself') in which all the detectible properties 'inhere', like pins in a pin-cushion.

Truth and necessity

In any account of the nature of truth, it is essential to distinguish between truths about abstractions, and truths about individual substances. If we take an abstraction, such as triangularity, the only predicates that can be truly ascribed to triangularity as such, are those that belong to its definition, or are deducible from it. So, if we define a triangle as *a plane figure with three angles and three sides*, we can say: 'A triangle is a plane figure', or: 'A triangle has three angles', or even: 'A triangle has fewer than five sides.' But it makes no sense to ascribe a particular shape or size to triangularity *in general*, or to ascribe a particular colour or weight to an abstract triangle of a definite shape or size.

Truths about abstractions are described as *analytic*, since it can be discovered by a process of analysis whether or not the predicate ascribed to the subject is a component of the definition of the subject. They are also *necessary* (necessarily true), since they are entirely self-contained: they risk no claims about what might or might not be the case in the real world, and so they cannot be falsified. *Contingent* truths, on the other hand, refer to concrete individuals, and are contingent upon what happens to be the case.

Most philosophers were in a position to distinguish between necessary and contingent truths. Leibniz, however, had spoilt the contrast between abstractions and concrete individuals, through his doctrine that an individual was a lowest species. At higher levels, he could still contrast the abstract concept with the individuals it covered. But the concept of a lowest species was a complete specification of all the properties of an individual – it was a 'complete concept', or 'individual notion'. Consequently Leibniz could not differentiate between what was necessarily true of an individual in virtue of its concept, and what was contingently true of it as a concrete individual. All truth had to be analytic, since to say that a predicate belonged to an individual subject was to say that it was part of the complete concept of that subject. As he wrote to Arnauld:

In every true, affirmative proposition, whether necessary or contingent, universal or singular, the notion of the predicate is somehow included in that of the subject – otherwise I do not know what truth is. (G ii 56)

It has often been held against Leibniz that, if all truth is analytic, then truths about individual substances must be as necessary as the truths of logic or of mathematics. Clearly Leibniz himself did not believe this, since he explicitly stated that his theory covered contingent as well as necessary truths. But it is important to see how he thought he could defend himself against the criticism, and where his defence falls down.

Leibniz defined a 'necessary' truth as one which could not have been otherwise, in that its opposite would imply a contradiction. So, it is necessary that a triangle has three sides, since the idea of a non-three-sided, three-sided figure is self-contradictory. By a 'contingent' truth, he meant one that could have been otherwise, in that its opposite would be non-contradictory, or logically possible. To use his own example, it is a contingent fact that Caesar crossed the Rubicon, since denying that he did so would not contradict anything else in his complete concept.

The difference between Leibniz and his critics lies in the question of what might or might not be contradicted by the idea of Caesar's turning back. In so far as the actual Caesar was the realisation of a complete concept including the predicate 'crossed the Rubicon', it is indeed contradictory to deny that *that* Caesar crossed the Rubicon. But this presupposes God's decision to actualise a Rubicon-crossing, rather than a non-Rubicon-crossing Caesar. And it is a trivial truth that, given God's final decision, any alternative would contradict it.

However, nothing has been said about the internal relations between the predicates constituting the subject. These cannot be *analytically* connected, since they are logically distinct. The infinitely many possible Caesars are nothing other than different combinations of separate predicates. If we imagine two Caesars with identical lists of predicates up to the point of decision at the Rubicon, their crossing it or not is just one more predicate, equally compatible with the rest. So when the actual Caesar in fact crossed the Rubicon, he was constrained not by the laws of logical necessity, but by God's decision as to which concept to actualise.

In fact, corresponding to every contingently true proposition, there will be a false one which is analytically true of another possible, but unactualised, subject, which differs only in that respect. Consequently, contingent truths are not true because they are analytic, but because the subjects of which they are analytically true are actual. And the difference between the actual and the merely possible involves the notion of existence, which, as we have seen, is not part of the concept of any created being.

The fact that God actualised this world rather than some other, cannot itself be an analytic truth. But given this one fundamental and infinitely complex contingent fact, all else is indeed analytic as part of it. Since God knows the concepts he has chosen in every detail, he himself has no use for knowledge in the form of propositions at all – he merely thinks the subject–concepts. And the more we mortals learn about individual subjects, the more we approach God's state in this respect.

In defining truth as analytic, Leibniz was trying to get away from the simplistic view that truth consisted in a correspondence between language and reality. But instead of abolishing the question of correspondence altogether, he shifted it over to the relation between *our* concepts, and concepts in the mind of God. And since he held that reality was nothing other than the realisation of a privileged set of divine concepts, Leibniz's thesis was much less radical than it might at first seem.

Discovery and proof

In common with most logicians of his time, Leibniz made a

sharp distinction between the logic of invention or discovery, and that of proof or judgement. Hitherto, the main successes of logic had been in formulating rules of proof, such as those used in the Aristotelian theory of the syllogism, and the axiomatic method of Euclidean geometry. Within certain narrow limits, given a particular hypothesis, it was now possible to prove whether or not that hypothesis was true. What was still completely lacking was a set of infallible rules for producing fruitful hypotheses. The best that philosophers had managed to devise were collections of common-sense tips – like avoiding prejudice, reducing problems to simpler sub-problems, trying alternative classifications of data and so on. Typical was Descartes' advice in the *Discourse on the Method* and the *Rules*.

Leibniz was dominated by the vision of a foolproof logic of discovery. His central idea was that the logic of discovery and that of judgement should be perfectly complementary. Since judgements of truth were always *analytic*, symmetry suggested that the process of discovery should be *synthetic*, or *combinatorial*, to use Leibniz's preferred term. In effect, it would be an extension of his student work on the art of combinations. However, he could not altogether eliminate the need for judgement and intuition, since the combinatory art was only a method for generating all the possible combinations of a set of concepts. It could not tell you *how* to analyse complex concepts into simples, nor could it tell you which combinations to prefer:

The human mind is analogous to a sieve: the process of thinking consists in shaking it until all the subtlest items pass through. Meanwhile, as they pass through, Reason acts as an inspector snatching out whatever seems useful. (C 170)

Moreover, the further mankind progressed towards a perfect language, the less scope there would remain either for the combinatory art or for rational judgement. Ultimately, we would have all the concepts we needed, and then we would only be able to utter explicitly analytic truths:

With the passage of time, certain operations which were once combinatorial will become analytic, after everyone has become familiar with my method of combination, which is within the grasp of even the dullest. This is why, with the gradual progress of the human species, it can come about, perhaps after many centuries, that no one will any more be praised for accuracy of judgement; for the analytic art (which is still virtually confined to mathematics in its correct and general use) will have become universal and applied to every type of matter through the introduction of a scientific notation or 'philosophical character' such as I am working on. Once this has been accepted, correct reasoning, given time for thought, will be no more praiseworthy than calculating large numbers without any error. Furthermore, if there is also a trustworthy catalogue of facts [a 'Universal Encyclopaedia'] . . . written in the same notation, together with the more important theorems . . . derived from the notation either alone or with observational data, it will come about that the art of combination will lose all its glory. (C 168)

We must now consider what grounds Leibniz had for believing that both analytic and synthetic reasoning could be reduced to purely mechanical operations. The key lies in what he called the *Principle of Identity*. This is the principle that a proposition is proved to be necessarily true if it either is itself an identical proposition, or can be reduced to one. An *identical* proposition is one in which the predicate is explicitly identical with or included in the subject. The simplest cases are of the form *a is a*, or *ab is a*. For example, 'Green is green', or 'Green grass is green.' Conversely, a proposition is necessarily false, or contradictory, if it is reducible to the form *a is not-a*.

The only legitimate procedure for *reducing* a proposition to an identical one is that of replacing a term by definitionally equivalent terms. So, the proposition 'Bachelors are rational' might be proved as follows:

1 For 'bachelors' substitute 'unmarried men', giving:
   'Unmarried men are rational.'
2 For 'men' substitute 'male humans', giving:
   'Unmarried male humans are rational.'
3 For 'humans' substitute 'rational animals', giving:
   'Unmarried male rational animals are rational.'

Now the predicate is explicitly included in the subject, and the proposition is proved.

In principle it would be possible to have a purely mechanical procedure for checking whether a proposition was identical, contradictory or as yet unproved. You merely had to *see* if the symbol on the right could be found on the left, and if so, whether either of them was preceded by a negation sign:

The only proposition of which the contrary implies a contradiction without one's being able to demonstrate it, is one of formal identity. The identity is formulated explicitly in the proposition, so it cannot be demonstrated – *demonstrated*, that is, made evident by reason and inferences. Here the identity can be made visible to the eye, so in this case it cannot be demonstrated. The senses make it evident that *a is a* is a proposition of which the opposite, *a is not-a*, formally implies a contradiction. But that which the senses make evident is indemonstrable. So the real, indemonstrable axioms are identical propositions. (C 186)

Although the checking process could in principle be done by a machine, human reason was still necessary for substituting definitions. To bypass human reason altogether would require a means of symbolising all the components of all complex concepts. In general terms, Leibniz's vision of a 'Universal Characteristic' to fulfil this function was very much in the tradition of Aristotle's tentative classification of concepts in the *Categories*; of the far more elaborate 'Great Art' of the medieval Spanish missionary Ramón Lull; of contemporary 'universal languages', especially John Wilkins's *Real Character and Philosophical Language*; and of the modern conception of a Thesaurus. What distinguished Leibniz's vision from the rest was his conviction that any adequate notation would have to be uncompromisingly numerical. He experimented with various systems. One model involved giving the simplest concepts a 'characteristic number', consisting of a pair of prime numbers, one positive and one negative. The characteristic number of a complex concept would be the *product* of the numbers of its components. To use his example (given in C 86–7): if 'animal' is $+ 13 - 5$ and 'rational' is $+ 8 - 7$, then 'man' will be $+ 104 - 35$ (that is, $+ 13 \times 8$, and $- 5 \times 7$). The reason why he represented the combination of concepts by multiplication rather than by addition should become clear in the next section. Meanwhile, it is important to understand why his notation included both positive and negative numbers.

A perfect notation must, of course, reflect the logical structure of the concepts themselves. It is tempting to assume that the complete concepts of individuals will be complexes of elementary components that are in themselves positive. So the individual concept of a particular physical object would be the sum of all its actual, positive properties – a particular shade of colour, its precise shape, size and weight and so on. Its complete concept would therefore be a sort of super-recipe, specifying absolutely every ingredient, and with infinite precision; and like other recipes, it would specify only what went in, and not what was left out. This was the approach that Locke adopted. However, Leibniz had three reasons for rejecting the assumption that all the components of individual complete concepts were positive simple predicates. The first arose from his belief that the created universe was differentiated from God only by the inclusion of an essential negative element (we shall come back to this in Chaper 6).

The second reason was that, if all the components of complex concepts were positive, there would be no way in which anything could be incompatible with anything else. Leibniz held that two concepts were incompatible only if there was some element in the one which was negated in the other, so that a contradiction of the form *a and not-a* could be derived from them. Since many concepts *are* mutually incompatible, for example those of the various possible Caesars, the constituents of complex concepts had somehow to include negation.

The third reason for rejecting a purely positive notation, was that it could represent only one aspect of an individual's complexity. As a concrete substance it might be nothing but the sum of its actual, positive characteristics. But as a lowest species, each individual also belonged to the realm of abstraction. As such, the individual was essentially the product of limitation or negation, and was what it was by virtue of its position within the hierarchy of abstract concepts. It was an act of faith on Leibniz's part that definitions of individuals arrived at by compounding concrete, simple predicates (a particular shape, size, colour and so on) would coincide with definitions reached by the repeated subdivision of abstract concepts (as in the Tree of Porphyry). But any notation capable of doing justice to the latter aspect had both to represent limitation and also to register the pedigree of each individual concept.

Leibniz's two-number notation was geared to fulfilling both requirements, even if rather clumsily. Limitation was symbolised by the negative number, and the pedigree would be traceable through the prime factors of the numbers, of which every genuinely distinct complex concept would have a unique combination.

The overwhelming disadvantage of the system was that numbers would rapidly become unmanageably large. It was possible to produce small-scale models of how it might work, but only by taking short runs of combinations of concepts arbitrarily assumed to be simple. The system could never be expanded to usable proportions.

An alternative approach which Leibniz envisaged, but never actually experimented with, was to give concepts a single number, but in *binary* notation. This way, even the most complex number might run to only a few millions; and the problem of incorporating the negative element was neatly overcome by interpreting all the 0s in any number as negative, and the 1s as positive. The main snag was that there would be no obvious way of registering how a large number could have been generated from a unique combination of smaller ones.

To sum up so far, Leibniz's long-term goal for logic involved a merging of the logic of discovery, the logic of judgement, and the rhetorical ideal of a perfect language. Given a binary notation and a set of combinatory rules, all possible thoughts could be generated and validated by purely mechanical means. In the mean time, we would have to content ourselves with improving the logic we already had.

Improving the syllogism

For most people, at least until well into the nineteenth century, logic *was* the theory of the syllogism. The theory is based on four general types of subject-predicate proposition, which can be interpreted as involving different permutations of 'all' and 'not'. They are as follows (with S representing the subject-term, and P the predicate-term):

1	*Universal Affirmative*	All S is P.	
2	*Universal Negative*	No S is P.	(All S is not-P.)
3	*Particular Affirmative*	Some S is P.	(Not all S is not-P.)
4	*Particular Negative*	Some S is not-P.	(Not all S is P.)

A syllogism consists of three propositions, two premises and a conclusion, such that the premises have one term in common (the 'middle term', = M), and the terms of the conclusion are the remaining two terms of the premises. This yields four possible combinations of positions of the terms (reversing the order of the premises makes no difference). These four combinations are known as the *syllogistic figures*, and are as follows:

Figure	1	2	3	4
Major Premise	M P	P M	M P	P M
Minor Premise	S M	S M	M S	M S
Conclusion	S P	S P	S P	S P

In every figure, each proposition can be of any of the four types, giving a grand total of 256 *moods*, or possible combinations of different types of proposition.

One of the tasks of the logician was to say which of the moods constituted valid arguments, and why. But the rules evolved for validating syllogisms were clumsy and arbitrary, and logicians could not even agree on a list of valid moods. The main problem was the ambiguity of the word 'some' in ordinary language. Take, for example, the following controversial syllogism:

> All one-horned animals are vertebrates;
> All unicorns are one-horned animals;
> Therefore some unicorns are vertebrates.

The premises are surely true, provided that the second one is understood as a definition; but there are two possible grounds for claiming that the conclusion is false, and that the syllogism is therefore invalid.

The first reason is that normally, when we say *some* individuals are something, we imply that others are not. Since *all* unicorns are vertebrates, this would make the conclusion false. The conclusion is true only if 'some' means 'at least some', leaving it open what is true of the rest.

The other reason for rejecting the syllogism would be that 'Some unicorns are vertebrates' can be interpreted as meaning 'There exists at least one vertebrate unicorn.' But this is false, since unicorns do not exist. The syllogism is valid only if the propositions beginning with 'all' and with 'some' have the same *existential import* – that is, if either both or neither of them imply that there actually exist members of the class in question.

Leibniz tackled the chaos of syllogistic theory as early as in his student thesis *On the Art of Combinations*. In this he tried to eliminate the arbitrariness of the rules for syllogistic validity, by structuring the theory round the permutations and combinations of 'all', 'not', and the subject, predicate and middle terms. As it stood, his project was over-ambitious and somewhat naïve in conception, but it was a promising start in the direction of making logic amenable to mathematical treatment. As far as conventional logic was concerned, he produced a symmetrical list of valid syllogisms by allowing six in each figure (including the one about unicorns).

His next step was to see that logic was essentially concerned with *concepts* or *classes* of things, and how they did or did not overlap. The distinction between subject and predicate, however important in grammar, had no ultimate significance for logic, since the two could always be swapped around. Instead of 'All men are mortal', you could say 'Mortality is an essential part of the human condition', or 'Mortals include all men among their number.' Besides, as we have already seen, Leibniz held that subjects, as lowest species, were really nothing other than highly complex predicates. So subject–predicate propositions merely asserted a certain relationship between the concepts or classes denoted by the two terms.

But, as Leibniz discovered, it makes a crucial difference to the relationship whether you are talking about concepts or about classes. For example, if the universal form 'All S is P' is interpreted in terms of concepts, it means that the concept S includes the concept P. Thus, in the proposition 'All men are animals', the concept 'man' includes the concept 'animal', in that man is by definition a rational animal. But if the proposition is about classes, it means that the class P includes the class S – to use the same example, men are a subclass of animals. The position with propositions containing 'some' is analogous, only more complicated because of the ambiguities already mentioned. The two interpretations are known as the *intensional* and the *extensional*. The conceptual interpretation is intensional, because it has to do with what you mean or intend by the concept; the class interpretation is extensional, because it has to do with the scope or extension of the class defined by the concept.

The next stage in Leibniz's thought was the one which made him the first true symbolic logician, and brought him to the very edge of abandoning traditional syllogistic logic altogether. We have already seen how he was searching for a way of notating concepts which would make their inner structure evident to the eye, and mechanically calculable. Given that logic was concerned with *relations between* concepts, he now hoped to make these relationships equally evident to the eye, and calculable.

The visual approach consisted in representing the extensions of classes geometrically. The simplest system Leibniz devised involved circles which either overlapped, or were entirely separate, or of which one included the other. They are now usually known as 'Venn diagrams', though John Venn himself (1834–1923) called them 'Eulerian', after Leonhard

69

Euler (1707–83), who presumably got the idea from his Leibnizian teacher, Johann Bernoulli (1667–1748). However, circles are usable only for the simplest cases, and Leibniz himself preferred a less immediate, but more versatile system, involving overlapping lines and brackets.

The second approach constituted an even more significant step towards modern logic, as also towards Leibniz's ambition of an arithmeticised universal characteristic. It consisted in representing the relationships between the intensions of concepts by a purely arithmetical notation, and in establishing the axioms of a formal calculus of deductive logic. He experimented with various different schemes, of which the most advanced are to be found in some private notes written during the 1690s.

In one of these papers, Leibniz used the symbol ' = ' to mean 'is the same as'; ' + ' for the combining of concepts; and ' – ' for the subtraction of a simpler concept from a more complex one. So, if A is 'man', B is 'rational' and C is 'animal', then 'A = B + C' means 'The concept of a man is the same as the concept of a rational animal'; and 'A – B = C' means 'If you subtract the qualification "rational" from the concept of a man, you are left with the concept of an animal.' He was well aware of the difference between his ' – ' and negation: the concept of a man with his rationality negated was a contradiction in terms (a non-rational rational animal); whereas the concept of a man with rationality subtracted merely reverted to that of an animal (G vii 232n.).

In a later paper, Leibniz dropped the subtraction sign as unnecessary, and altered the ' + ' to '⊕', to show that it was different from the ' + ' of arithmetic. For example, his calculus had as an axiom 'A + A = A', meaning that to add the same qualification a second time made no further difference to a concept. But in arithmetic, A + A = 2A.

Leibniz did not in fact get very far with his logical calculus.

Clearly, what he envisaged was something like the system finally produced by George Boole (1815–64). Boole's calculus was a purely formal deductive system, which could do everything that syllogistic logic could do, while avoiding its ambiguities and apparent arbitrariness. But although Leibniz's failure to arrive at Boolean algebra itself was a near miss, he had an even nearer miss from the twentieth-century concept of *truth-tables*.

When Leibniz saw that his '⊕' was not the ' + ' of arithmetic, he failed to consider the possibility of its being some other mathematical operator. This was despite the fact that he himself had previously notated 'A⊕B' as 'AB', which is an alternative for 'A × B' in algebra. Now, if we symbolise being-a-member-of-a-class by '1', and not-being-a-member by '0', we can then draw up a simple table defining membership of the class A⊕B in terms of membership of the classes A and B. The only circumstance in which something is a member of A⊕B is when it is a member of A and is a member of B:

A	B	A⊕B
0	0	0
0	1	0
1	0	0
1	1	1

If we now interpret the 0 and 1 as binary numbers, it is clear that '⊕' is not the ' + ' of arithmetic, which would have given: 0, 1, 1, 10 in the third column, since in binary, $0 + 1 = 1$, $1 + 0 = 1$ and $1 + 1 = 10$. In fact it is equivalent to multiplication: $0 \times 0 = 0, 0 \times 1 = 0, 1 \times 0 = 0, 1 \times 1 = 1$. This is why logicians call the class defined by the combination of two concepts their 'logical product'.

If we now ask what the mathematical ' + ' is equivalent to in logic, we are faced with the problem that no meaning has been given to symbols other than 0 and 1 by themselves: an individual either is or is not a member of a given class. The logical notation has no use for 'numbers' greater than 1. However, if we imagine a degenerate binary arithmetic with only the two numbers 0 and 1, adding 1 to 1 will bring us round again to 0 (like a rotary switch, with only the two positions, 'on' and 'off'). The operation can be represented by the following table:

A	B	A + B
0	0	0
0	1	1
1	0	1
1	1	0

Translated into logical terms, we have the operator 'or', in the everyday, exclusive sense of 'one or other, but not both' (in this sense it would be wrong to say, 'Leeds is either in England or in Yorkshire', since it happens to be in both).

Leibniz came very close to defining this function when he introduced the notion of 'incommunicating' classes. They were such that a member of a pair of incommunicating classes was a member of one or the other, but not of both. However, although the function was essential for his calculus, he never got as far as representing it symbolically. If he had done so, he might have arrived at a general logic of 'either/or', which could have served equally for his own 'either a member of a class or not'; for the 'either true or false' of truth-tables; or for the 'either carrying an electric current or not', which is the basis of the modern computer.

5 Metaphysics

Philosophical method

Leibniz regularly referred to his metaphysical theory as a *system* – in particular, the *System of Pre-Established Harmony*. This raises the question of whether he intended to stress the systematic character of his metaphysics, or whether he merely meant 'system' in the sense of 'theory', as when we talk of 'the Copernican system', for instance. Many commentators have assumed that Leibniz's metaphysics was systematic in the former sense, despite the fact that his actual writings are a complete jumble in comparison with the systematic treatises of contemporaries such as Spinoza, Hobbes or Malebranche. The question of the systematic character of Leibniz's philosophy is an important one, and to settle it we must distinguish between his ambition and his achievement.

It will be obvious from the previous chapter that Leibniz's ideal must have been a fully deductive system. Indeed, when he was about forty, he seems to have found his philosophical ideas suddenly falling into place, and he went as far as to claim that everything followed from the Principle of Identity (see p. 62 above) and the Principle of Sufficient Reason (the principle that there must be some reason why anything is as it is rather than otherwise). But he never showed how the rest of his system followed from those two principles, and the nearest he ever came to producing a systematic exposition of his philosophy as a whole was in a number of short summaries written at various times during his life – in particular, the *Discourse on Metaphysics* (1686), the *New System* (1695) and the so-called *Monadology* (1714).

Although these tracts are by no means devoid of reasoned argument, they read more like dogmatic creeds or manifestos, and they certainly fall far short of showing how his various philosophical tenets are supposed to come together as a deductive system. Those who stress the systematic character of Leibniz's philosophy tend to appeal to the structure that they, as commentators, can detect in his writings, especially in his private notes. For example, in his *Critical Exposition of the Philosophy of Leibniz* (1900), Lord Russell dismissed most of Leibniz's correspondence and publications as obsequious panderings to aristocratic patrons. Russell used Leibniz's unpublished jottings as the basis for 'a reconstruction of the system which Leibniz *should have* written' (my italics). But it is surely an extreme measure to ignore precisely those writings to which Leibniz gave his seal of approval, and to base one's interpretation on his tentative speculations. In fact much of what Leibniz published seemed strange even to his contemporaries, and it was hardly calculated to ingratiate him with anyone. It is clear that Leibniz aspired to a system, but the system remained half formed in his mind.

The actual Leibniz was nearly always *in dialogue* – with real live opponents in the course of his voluminous correspondence; with imaginary interlocutors when writing in explicit dialogue form (for example, in his *New Essays*, a lengthy dialogue between a Leibnizian and a Lockean); and with himself in his private notes. It may be that, in the light of his hankering after a system, the open-endedness of dialogue seemed to him a second best. On the other hand, his great philosophical hero was Plato, and Plato never used anything but the dialogue form. Both believed that truth ultimately rested in the logical relationships between hierarchically structured objective concepts, and both believed that the most appropriate method for us to discover the truth was the dialectical method. Once the system of concepts had been traced back to its source, it would in principle be possible to expound it deductively. But in practice such a system would always remain beyond the reach of human intelligence, since the apex of the hierarchy of concepts was nothing other than God himself.

Leibniz was perfectly willing to admit that he did not have a complete system. As he wrote to the Paris Academician, Gilles des Billettes in 1696:

My system . . . is not a complete body of philosophy, and I do not claim to have a reason for everything that other people have thought they can explain. Progress must be gradual to be assured. (G vii 451)

As we shall see, it was one of the main theses of his philosophy that objective truth is the summation of the different viewpoints of all individuals. Quite properly, he applied the thesis to the philosophical disputes in which he himself was involved:

Most philosophical schools are largely right in what they assert, but not so much in what they deny. (G iii 607)

Consideration of this system [of mine] makes it evident that when one comes down to the basics, one finds that most philosophical schools have more of the truth than one would have believed . . . They come together as at a centre of perspective, from which an object (confused if looked at from any other position) displays its regularity and the appropriateness of its parts. The commonest failing is the sectarian spirit in which people diminish themselves by rejecting others. (G iv 523–4)

Leibniz's use of dialogue, far from obscuring some supposed underlying system, in fact provides the key to the genuine structural unity of his writings, both public and private. He believed that in most disputes each side had part of the truth and was wrong only in failing to recognise what was true in the opposing position. Truth was therefore best served, not by adding facts or arguments to one side or another, but by finding a framework which would maximise the compatibility of the various points of view. His philosophical system was intended to function as just such a framework; and in practice its justification was its success in reconciling philosophical opposites, not its deducibility from a few self-evident premises. Leibniz's system was a 'system of harmony' not merely in the sense that it postulated a harmony of the universe, but also in that he intended it to bring about a 'harmony of the philosophers', as he put it in his student days.

Scholastics versus moderns

During the period when Leibniz was developing his philosophy, it was comparatively rare for the professional, scholastic philosophers to pay much attention to the 'modern' philosophy of amateurs such as Bacon, Descartes or Hobbes. With the passage of time, the traditionalists felt themselves increasingly under threat, but they tended to retaliate with violent abuse or attempts at censorship, rather than by any sort of compromise. This is hardly surprising, since for their part the modern philosophers were unanimous in their wholesale rejection of scholasticism. Their various schemes for starting completely afresh from indubitable axioms, crystal-clear definitions and the evidence of the senses, and their rejection of traditional terminology as meaningless obfuscation, almost wholly precluded the possibility of finding any common ground between the two approaches. With the benefit of hindsight, we can now see that the moderns were not wholly successful in escaping from the traditional modes of thought which dominated their education and culture. But it was their conscious attitude that mattered: they all saw themselves as at war with the scholastics.

From an early age, Leibniz felt himself torn between the two camps. He loved the subtle complexity, the precision and the systematic approach of the scholastic writers he had been brought up on. In particular, he had a life-long admiration for the leading Spanish scholastic, Francisco Suárez (1548–1617). On the other hand, he was also attracted by the simplicity and explanatory power of modern mathematics and the mechanistic picture of the universe. In his early youth, he was for a while completely converted to the new atomic theory as expounded by the French philosopher, Pierre Gassend or Gassendi (1592–1655), and Hobbes. However, he soon moved to a middle position in which he recognised merits in both the new and the old. From then on, he devoted considerable efforts to mediating between the two factions, by developing a conceptual and theoretical framework they could both accept.

Leibniz believed that the scholastics were at fault, not in their respect for tradition as such, but in allowing their traditionalism to become so ossified and inward-looking that they were incapable of absorbing new techniques and discoveries. Conversely, the moderns threw the baby out with the bathwater in their wholesale rejection of scholasticism. It was easy to poke fun at the logic-chopping and clumsy neologisms of university metaphysics, but its technical terms and distinctions provided a valuable means for conceptualising certain unavoidable metaphysical issues. Wilful renunciation of scholastic terminology had lulled the moderns into glossing over problems at the very roots of their philosophies.

Leibniz's usual formula for mediating in any dispute thrown up by the modern philosophy was to show that it arose from neglect of traditional metaphysical concepts. He believed that scholastic terminology could generally be used to express a deeper theory in terms of which both sides could be seen as right in what they asserted, and wrong only in feeling themselves threatened by the insights of their opponents. Obviously this technique was most directly applicable within metaphysics itself, and we shall come across a number of examples during the course of the present chapter. But Leibniz also used it in other contexts. For instance, the framework for his theory of space was supplied by the traditional concepts of *substance*, *accident* and *relation*. Similarly, his Principle of the Identity of Indiscernibles, which he used in scientific contexts (as when he denied that there could be identical atoms – see p. 56 above), presupposed scholastic theories of individuation, and concepts such as that of a lowest species. Again, in theology he evolved the typically scholastic conception of a 'substantial connector' (*vinculum substantiale*), in order to reconcile Catholic, Lutheran and Calvinist positions in relation to the dogma of transubstantiation.

Cartesians versus atomists

Within the non-scholastic philosophy of the mid-seventeenth century, the two main rival accounts of the nature of material substance in general were those of the Cartesians and of the atomists (especially Gassendi). Cartesianism was hardly known in Germany while Leibniz was a student, so it made all the more impression on him during his stay in Paris. For a while he was almost totally absorbed in Descartes' writings, and although he did not emerge as a Cartesian, his sympathetic critique of crucial aspects of Cartesianism played a significant role in the development of his own philosophical system.

The main difference between the two theories of matter was this: For the Cartesians, matter was essentially a continuous, homogeneous quantity, and its division into apparently distinct physical objects was something requiring explanation. For the atomists, matter consisted essentially in discrete bits separated by empty space, and it was its cohesion into apparently homogeneous physical objects that required explanation. As we shall see, Leibniz believed that neither position alone was correct, and that it was essential to appeal to certain scholastic principles and concepts in order to reconcile the apparently conflicting demands for continuity and discreteness.

Descartes, true to his profound anti-scholasticism, wanted to escape as far as possible from what he saw as mere quibbling about elementary scholastic terms, such as *substance*, *accident*, *essence*, *matter* and *form*. His radically simplified categorisation of reality divided it into two things: *thought* (or consciousness) and *extension* in space. Every item of the world as we knew it was a *mode*, or particular manifestation, either of thought or of extension. Our beliefs, intentions, emotional attitudes and conscious perceptions were modes of thought; and the qualities genuinely belonging to physical objects themselves, and not just to our perceptions of them, were modes of extension.

But since the only real properties of matter were the spatial or geometrical ones of shape, size and motion (or change of relative position), Descartes could not accommodate any absolute distinction between matter itself and the space occupied by matter. The notion of empty space was a contradiction in terms, since matter was not distinguished from it by anything such as substantiality, mass or solidity. For Descartes, the material universe was essentially nothing other than an infinite sea of homogeneous, extended matter.

However, in order to ensure some connection between his metaphysics and the world of ordinary experience, Descartes had to explain how his essentially homogeneous matter could give rise to the variety of things like stones, water, air, plants and animals. His immediate solution was to say that matter was divided into corpuscles of three different orders of size: the largest made up tangible solids and liquids; the medium

ones formed air and volatile spirits; and the smallest constituted an all-pervading ether, which filled even what we would
normally think of as a vacuum.

But this only moved the problem one stage back. Since
matter was strictly homogeneous, meaning had to be given to
the notion of a particular mathematical point belonging to one
corpuscle rather than to another; or of a particular volume of
space constituting a single large corpuscle, rather than a
densely packed collection of smaller ones. Descartes' answer
was in terms of the only other available intrinsic property of
matter, namely *motion*. His criterion for saying that a given
volume constituted an individual corpuscle distinct from the
surrounding matter, was that the whole volume *moved together*. In effect, he pictured the universe as like an infinite
tank of water, containing frozen lumps of various shapes and
sizes: the ice was of the same nature as the water, and differed
from it only in the mutual cohesion of its parts.

Leibniz's objection was that it made no sense to say that one
part of space was in motion relative to another, unless they
were already distinguished from each other. In the ice example, there *are* criteria for a piece of ice having moved in water,
since ice is intrinsically different from water in many ways: it
is solid, and colder and refracts light differently. But if the
only difference were the cohesion of the ice when it moved,
then there would be no specifiable difference between the
state of affairs in the tank before and after the supposed
motion. In accordance with the Principle of the Identity of
Indiscernibles, there would have been no change, and therefore no motion. The very concept of motion presupposes intrinsically distinct things relative to which motion can take
place. Consequently, intrinsic difference cannot, without circularity, depend on motion. Descartes' theory of matter col-
lapses for lack of an inherent basis of variegation (in scholastic

terms, a 'principle of individuation') to differentiate one part of matter from another.

The atomists avoided Descartes' problem over variegation by conceiving solid atoms as intrinsically different from the surrounding empty space. Given atoms of different shapes and sizes, it was not difficult in principle to imagine how their various combinations might give rise to all the variety of the world as we know it. Their problem, in Leibniz's view, was to explain *cohesion*. Suppose we have a collection of atoms: the problem is to give an account of the difference between their constituting a single, solid object, and their being merely a heap or aggregate, like a pile of sand. If atoms were to be the sole constituents of material reality, the atomists could not appeal to any occult 'cohesive forces', or to quasi-material 'gluons' sticking them together, as in some modern physical theories. One solution was to say that the atoms of solid objects held together by interlocking hooks and eyes, like Velcro, or three-dimensional puzzles.

Leibniz's objection was that, far from explaining cohesion, this account presupposed it, in the form of the internal cohesion of the atoms themselves. If the atomists said that atoms held together because they were composed of smaller atoms with hooks and eyes, the process would go on to infinity. So they had to say that atoms were *intrinsically* indivisible (as implied by the very name ἄ-τομον, meaning 'uncuttable'). But this made cohesion an ultimate, and hence inexplicable, property of nature.

Not only would cohesion be inexplicable, but, in Leibniz's view, the point at which it was appealed to would be entirely arbitrary. He held (wrongly, it would now seem) that size is purely relative. Consequently, if it is a puzzle how, say, the moon holds together, or how a cannon-ball holds together, then it must equally be a puzzle how a material atom holds together. However small an object may be, it is possible to define two halves of it; and it can always then be asked whether they form a whole, or whether the two halves just happen to be resting in perfect contact with each other. It is impossible for a pure atomic theory to account for the difference between these two states of affairs.

Leibniz claimed that both the Cartesians and the atomists had gone astray in what he called 'the labyrinth of the composition of the continuum' (G vi 65). The Cartesians took continuity as their point of departure, but could not succeed in crystallising discrete objects out of it. The atomists postulated discrete atoms, but could not explain their composition into continuous wholes. Leibniz believed that each were right in what they asserted, and that the material world was *both* a continuum, *and* composed of atomic units.

As he saw it, the problem of the composition of the continuum was this: if its atomic units were small enough to be genuine units (that is, logically indivisible, unlike material atoms, which were indivisible only by arbitrary assumption), then they would have to be mathematical points. But since mathematical points had no dimensions, they could not contain any substance, so as to be real in their own right. Besides, even if there could be such things as real mathematical points, they certainly could not generate matter by being laid next to each other, since any number of points together collapse into a single point. In short, anything small enough to be part of a continuum would be too small to be an ultimate building-block of matter.

In his early days, Leibniz thought he could get round the problem by appealing to the scholastic concept of the *flowing* of a point. His idea was that, if a point was in continuous motion, it would at any instant be moving away from where it was, and would therefore be occupying fractionally more than the zero space of a stationary point. Moving points might therefore be large enough to function as the elements of three-dimensional objects. Moreover, since motion was a positive characteristic of things, it might endow points with some sort of real existence – unlike the utter nothingness of a static mathematical point.

So Leibniz's first solution was to say that the essence of matter was not Descartes' extension, or the atomists' solidity, but *motion*: every part of matter was composed of infinitely many continuously moving points. However, this position was inherently unsatisfactory, since it suffered from the very same mistake that Leibniz had accused Descartes of: motion presupposes that which moves, and therefore cannot constitute its essence. Motion had to be grounded in something else; and whatever that something was, would have to be capable of existing at a point.

As we saw in Chapter 3, Leibniz criticised Descartes for failing to see that motion had to be grounded in *energy*. Applied to his own theory, this led him to the conclusion that it was energy that existed at a point and constituted the essence of matter. Other thinkers saw motion or energy as something extra, added to the world after it had already been created (like a clock wound up by its maker). For Leibniz, the world consisted of nothing but point-particles of energy permanently expressed in motion. This energy was the source not only of the activities of physical objects (in particular, kinetic energy), but also of their passive aspect, or matter itself, which just *was* the energy to resist penetration or acceleration, and to react to applied forces (see pp. 43 f.).

In short, Leibniz's way out of the labyrinth of the composition of the continuum was to see the world of continuously extended matter as secondary and derivative. He realised that he could not explain matter and space without circularity, unless he derived them from beings of a different category. His infinity of energy-points fitted the bill nicely, since they were themselves neither material, nor, strictly speaking, even spatial. The details of how Leibniz thought matter was derived from energy will be filled out in the course of the rest of the present chapter.

Mechanists versus vitalists

At its sharpest, the dispute between mechanists and vitalists was over the choice of a single model for understanding the whole of nature. Extreme mechanists, such as Hobbes, interpreted everything, including biological and psychological phenomena, as the products of underlying mechanisms operating in accordance with deterministic laws. Extreme vitalists, such as Leibniz's close friend Francis Mercury van Helmont, tended to interpret everything, including the functioning of everyday machinery, as due to the operations of invisible, goal-directed organic principles. For the former, the universe was a huge machine, of which the parts were also machines; for the latter it was a huge animal, of which the parts were also animals.

Descartes was strongly inclined towards extreme mechanism, but he baulked at including reason and consciousness within the mechanist model. His compromise was to allow the laws of mechanics complete sway over the realm of matter, but to take the human soul right out of nature. As we saw (see pp. 38 f.), Leibniz criticised him for wanting to eat his cake and have it. If he was really serious about exempting the soul from the laws of nature, he would be committed to denying that the soul could act upon the body at all, even though it might still be indirectly influenced by the body through consciousness of what was happening to it.

Leibniz was as convinced as Descartes of the universality of the laws of mechanics, and of the futility of vitalist explanations of natural phenomena, but he could not fudge the issue of our role in nature as Descartes had done. He firmly accepted the conclusion that, since we are part of nature, we must be subject to its laws like anything else. Any special status that humans might have in comparison with animals would have to be understood at a moral rather than at a metaphysical level (see Chapter 6). But this made it all the more urgent for him to explain how human action, and indeed that of all other living organisms, was to be reconciled with universal mechanism.

Leibniz's solution was not to restrict the scope of mechanism in any way, but to make *all* mechanical explanation ultimately dependent on a metaphysical version of vitalism. As he wrote to Arnauld:

Nature must always be explained mathematically and mechanically, provided it is remembered that the principles themselves, or laws of mechanics or force, do not depend on mathematical extension alone, but on certain metaphysical reasons. (G ii 58)

He had a number of grounds for denying the sufficiency of mechanical explanations. One relatively trivial reason was that the laws of mechanics could not be used to explain themselves. If there were to be any explanation of why precisely this set of laws held rather than some other possible set, it would have to be found outside mechanics itself, in metaphysics or theology for example, in that the actual laws were chosen by God as the best. But many philosophers would have agreed with Leibniz on this, and it does nothing to account for the radical consequences which he alone drew from the insufficiency of mechanics.

Of much deeper significance for his philosophy was his analysis of the nature of mechanical interaction itself. We have already looked at his scientific grounds for denying real interaction, and for concluding that all action must be spontaneous (see p. 43), but he also had a metaphysical argument for the same conclusion. This was that, although we tend to picture force as a *thing* which is transferred from one body to another (like a baton in a relay race), really it is not a thing at all, but only a quality or state of things. Consequently, a force cannot literally be transferred from one body to another, any more than a colour, a headache or a smile.

It is a serious misconception to think of causation simply in terms of a chain of influences passing on from one individual object to another. Even in the case of balls ricocheting off each other on a snooker table, we must never forget that their motions are permanently dependent on an infinity of other considerations, such as the characteristics of the table, the lie of the felt, air currents, all the gravitational forces acting on them and so on. In fact, the resultant motion of a particular ball is more like the expression of the solution to an infinitely complex equation, than like receiving the baton in a relay race. Leibniz was quite right to interpret the laws of mechanics, not as laws governing the amount of force transferred from one colliding body to another, but as elegant mathematical formulae governing the evolution of whole complex systems from their state at one time to their state at the next.

At the everyday level, we quite properly see such systems as involving interactions between different bodies. But if, strictly speaking, all action is really spontaneous, then the law-guided evolution of the system as a whole must ultimately derive from the internal evolution of each individual substance. In other words, there are two different dimensions to the changes in an individual's states: its spontaneous development from within its own nature, and the adaptation of that development to the harmony of the total system of which it is a part. Of the two dimensions, the former is more fundamental, given that the part is prior to the whole. But since God selected individuals for actualisation only with a view to the role they would play within a total system, the two dimensions are really interdependent.

Typically, Leibniz chose to express his position in the terminology of the Aristotelian-scholastic tradition. The two dimensions of things were essentially *active* and *passive* – things were active in so far as their development was spontaneous; passive in so far as it was determined by the requirements of the surrounding system. Leibniz identified the two dimensions with the traditional *form* (active) and *matter* (passive). From a scholastic point of view, it was then utterly orthodox to say that the two aspects were complementary, and that every earthly substance had to have both.

In the case of living organisms, the scholastics had identified the form with the soul: as the *essence* of the living thing, the form must be its principle of life. In the case of man, his form was his rationality, or rational soul; in the case of animals it was the capacity for sensation, or the 'sensitive' soul; in the case of plants it was their principle of organic life, or 'vegetative' soul. Leibniz's crucial step was to say that there was no difference in *kind* between the forms of living substances and those of everything else: everything had a form as well as matter, and thereby had a vital principle as the ultimate source of its spontaneous activity.

This, in general terms, was how Leibniz thought he could reconcile mechanism and vitalism. Absolutely everything was subject to the deterministic laws of mechanics in virtue of interaction with other substances. But the capacity to interact depended ultimately on spontaneous change, which arose from forms or vital principles. However, in order to understand more precisely how the two aspects were supposed to be connected, we must look now at Leibniz's resolution of yet another metaphysical conflict.

Phenomenalists versus realists

A phenomenalist is one who believes that nothing exists apart from perceivers and their perceptions (or 'phenomena'). A realist, in this context, means someone who believes that there also exists a real world underlying our perceptions. Leibniz had an ingenious idea for reconciling these two apparently contradictory metaphysical theories. What he did was to start from an unambiguously phenomenalist position, and then to reconstruct a realist picture of the universe on the basis of his conception of forms as vital principles capable of something analogous to perception.

Unlike later phenomenalists, Leibniz did not rest his case on the unknowability of some supposedly more real world lying behind the one we are immediately aware of in experience. He preferred to argue directly that the material world of experience had two essential features which consigned it to the realm of appearance rather than of reality.

The first feature was the same as had led Plato to reject the reality of matter, namely that it was essentially in a state of *becoming*, not of *being*:

The objects of perception, and in general all compounds or what one might call artificial substances, are in a flux, and in a state of becoming rather than of being. (E 445)

As we have seen, Leibniz held that the essence of matter was energy, and that everything was always moving, since energy, in the form of kinetic energy, could be actualised only through motion. Since things were *essentially* in motion, they had to differ from things at rest, at every instant of their existence. The difference was that, like a 'flowing point' (see p. 82), a moving object would always be already entering its next position – it both did and did not occupy a precisely defined space, unlike a stationary object, which occupied a space exactly equal to itself. But this was a contradiction. Like a blurred photograph, it could belong only to the realm of representation or appearance. Reality itself could not be blurred, but had to be precisely what it was and nothing else.

The other feature of matter which made it merely phenomenal was the fact that it was irreducibly composite. Leibniz held that compounds were not real in themselves, but only in virtue of their components (see p. 53 f.); and as he had argued against the atomists (see p. 81), the parts of spatially extended, material compounds had also to be extended, and therefore themselves capable of further subdivision, and so on to infinity. The only way out of the infinite regress was to postulate genuine unities, or 'monads' (from the Greek μόνας, meaning 'unit'), which would not be *parts* of matter, but on which matter would depend in some other way. In Leibniz's terminology, monads were not parts, but 'requisites' of matter. Granted that matter consisted of appearances, its existence would have to depend on perceivers to which it appeared. Leibniz's theory was that monads, as principles of energy and life, were the perceivers on which material bodies ultimately depended:

Extension, mass and motion are no more things than images in mirrors, or rainbows in clouds . . . Anything in nature apart from perceivers and their perceptions is invented by us, and we struggle with chimeras created by our own minds, as if with ghosts. (G ii 281)

We normally understand the world as consisting of objects of perception separate from and common to different perceivers. Leibniz held that such objects are only mental constructs. For example, if we imagine a number of people looking at a solid cube, they will all have different perspectives on it. None will have a perceptual image answering to the geometrical description of a cube as a solid with six squares at right angles to each other. Leibniz's phenomenalism commits him to denying that there is a real cube of that description over and above the various perceptual images. We may refer our perceptions to a supposed objective cube, but this cube is only a mental construct, since it has properties no one sees as such. It may be *as if* the individual perspectives were derived from an external cube, but this will be no more than a fictional extrapolation from the individual perspectives.

The fiction is, however, a useful one, since the specification of the cube is encapsulated in a neat mathematical formula from which the details of every possible perspective can be straightforwardly derived. But all that matters is the mathematical formula itself – a purely mental thing. Once we have that, there is no need for some extra-mental cube itself in which the formula has a physical embodiment. The reason why our perceptions are coherent and orderly is not that they depend on supernumerary, unperceiving substances, but because they were chosen by God with a view to maximising their mutual harmony in accordance with mathematical principles.

The only channel of communication between different perceivers is through their perceived bodies. If one person is in communication with another, it is by means of speaking, gesturing and touching, and by means of hearing, watching and feeling the other person. It is precisely this importance of the perceived body that leads us to conceive of the body as the most immediate reality, and the conscious soul as somehow secondary, and hidden within the body. For instance, Descartes' theory of the pineal gland as the seat of the soul suggested that the soul was *in* a particular part of the body, though in a way which put it magically just beyond the reach of the neurosurgeon's scalpel. But for Leibniz, the unreality of the body meant that the soul or monad could not be literally *in* it. It was the body, as phenomenon, that was in the soul, rather than the other way round. However, given the everyday fiction that bodies are real, we can talk *as if* souls inhabited them, even though they are no more *in* bodies than they are *in* letters, pictures, telephones or any other means of communication.

The next question is: Which bodies are animated? Since Leibniz identified monads or souls with forms, a first answer is that all parts of matter that exhibit form are animated. Unlike the scholastics, however, Leibniz was not prepared to attribute forms to purely material objects. As principles of unity, he restricted them to genuinely unitary wholes, or *organisms*.

A material object, even one which has deliberately been given a certain form by a human craftsman, is not a genuine whole, since it is no more than the sum of its parts. If you dismantle a table, you have the parts of a table, and can put them back together again. But if you dismantle a person, you end up with parts of a *corpse*; and reassembling the parts will give you only a complete corpse, and not a person. What distinguishes a person from a corpse is his being a living organism. And this distinction does not depend on the presence of some extra ingredient, for example an immaterial soul inserted by God at conception, or the electrical energy that Frankenstein added to his monster. Such an addition would be just another *part*, and the whole would still be no more than the sum of its parts.

What makes an organism an organic whole is the way in which its parts are interconnected. For Leibniz, this was not simply a question of co-ordinated activity and mutual responsiveness, since these could also be found in sophisticated machinery. In his view, the defining characteristic of an organism was that each part depended for its very identity on its relation to that particular whole. Unlike human artefacts, which had essentially interchangeable parts made of apparently homogeneous substance, the parts of an organism were peculiar to the organism of which they were parts. This meant that each part had somehow to be capable of reflecting the complex unity of the whole organism. In other words, it also had to be a complex organism with its own organic parts, and so on to infinity. Apart from the reference to infinity, this is strikingly suggestive of modern biological theories as to the specificity of bodily organs and cells. As Leibniz himself put it in the *Monadology*:

So every organic body of a living being is a sort of God-made machine, or natural robot, which infinitely excels all man-made robots. For human skill cannot make machines of which all their parts are machines. For example, the tooth of a brass cog-wheel has parts or segments which are not themselves man-made and no longer have any mechanical role in the functioning of the wheel. But machines of nature, that is to say living bodies, are still machines in their smallest parts, right down to infinity. It is that which makes the difference between nature and art, or rather between God's art and ours.(§64)

But if there are to be organic bodies within organic bodies, there must also be perceptions within perceptions, since bodies are ultimately nothing but perceptions. However, when we perceive bodies, we do not consciously perceive the microscopic organisms of which they are composed – so we must perceive them unconsciously. This consideration led Leibniz to formulate a distinction, remarkable for his time, between the conscious and the unconscious. Consciousness he termed 'apperception', and unconscious perceptions he described as 'little perceptions'. His idea was that little perceptions are components of our conscious perceptions, but ones that are not separately (or 'distinctly') perceived in themselves. For example, we cannot hear the distant roar of the sea unless we hear every single drop of water, even though the individual drops are below the threshold of conscious perception. Again, we feel the weight of our bodies as a single impression, even though it is really the resultant of an infinity of individually indistinguishable gravitational forces emanating from the whole of the rest of the universe. In effect, 'little perceptions' are nothing more than the unconscious registration of the active forces of other bodies. Leibniz is using a psychological model to account for the principle that everything is influenced by everything else.

From a metaphysical point of view, the doctrine of organisms within organisms gives a means of filling out the reality of phenomenal bodies. Although we can talk as if bodies contained souls, it makes no sense to say *where* the soul is within the body. It is not even like a pea rattling around inside an otherwise empty pod, since the relation between body and soul is logical rather than spatial. But if bodies are in fact colonies of smaller bodies, then there must be as many souls 'inside' the higher-level bodies as there are smaller bodies, and the scope for the indeterminacy of the position of each soul is confined to the volume of these smaller bodies. If the smaller bodies are in their turn colonies of yet smaller bodies, and so on to infinity, then it is impossible to define a portion of a body so small that it will not include an infinity of souls. Literally, every specifiable part of the phenomenal body is backed up by infinitely many real substances. If, as realism maintains, the reality of phenomena is to consist in their correspondence with underlying real substances, then Leibniz's phenomena are as real as any realist could demand.

At a purely empirical level, Leibniz found dramatic confirmation of his approach in what had been discovered through the newly invented microscope. Examination of the human body revealed all sorts of hitherto invisible components which seemed to have a life of their own: spermatozoa, blood corpuscles and other cells. In view of this, it was natural for him to see the human body as basically an organic colony of microscopic living beings. And if that were true of everyday bodies, one might suppose that the microscopic animals constituting them would in their turn be colonies of yet smaller ones, and so on.

So far, Leibniz's theory accounts for the reality of the *organic* bodies in our experience. However, it would be absurd to picture a world in which all our perceptions of *living* beings were grounded in reality, but in which all the surrounding inanimate objects were mere appearances in the mind. So Leibniz was more or less forced into maintaining that they too were collections of living beings, though not such as to form organic wholes. Material objects were mere 'aggregates' of organisms, like banks of living animal tissues in a laboratory. Leibniz thought he had empirical confirmation of this too, from microscopic examination of chalk, which showed it to be a mass of shells and skeletons of tiny sea creatures. So, although matter was in itself only a phenomenon, it was a 'well-founded' phenomenon, in that it was constructed from bodies of organisms, analysable in their turn as perceptions of real, living beings.

The idea of a hierarchy of organisms within organisms established more than just their reality. Since organisms were 'machines of nature', it explained how, at every level, there were always sub-mechanisms available for mediating interactions. In addition, the infinite complexity of monads made it possible for Leibniz to claim that each one registered the influence of, or 'mirrored', not only its own body, but the whole of the universe. Its perceptual state *was* the whole phenomenal world from a particular point of view, so it was in principle possible to read off everything else from it. Finally, given knowledge of the laws of nature, one could then calculate every future event, and given also that everything retained traces of all past influences (the conservation of information), it would even be possible to unravel the past history of the universe.

Had Leibniz lived a little later, he might have expressed his theory in the more neutral terms of field dynamics. But in his day, the vitalist and psychological model was the only one available for conceptualising reality as something other than material, atomic and inert. Terms like 'life', 'soul' and 'perception' were all he had for describing co-ordinated energy and activity without consciousness. So we should not read too much into the more fanciful expositions of his philosophy, such as the following almost poetic passage from the *Monadology*:

There is a world of creatures, living beings, animals, substantial forms, souls in the very smallest part of matter. Each bit of matter can be thought of as a garden full of plants or as a pond full of fish – except that every branch of a plant, every part of an animal's body, every drop of the liquids they contain is in its turn another such garden or pond. And although the earth and the air occupying the spaces between the plants in the garden, or the water occupying the space between the fishes in the pond, is not itself a plant or a fish, yet they contain still more of them, only mostly too small to be visible. Thus there is nothing uncultivated, sterile or dead in the universe – no chaos or confusion, except in appearance. It is rather as a pond appears from a distance, when you can see a confused motion and milling around, so to speak, of the fishes in the pond, but without being able to make out the individual fishes themselves. One sees from this how every living body has a dominant substantial form which is the soul in the animal; but the members of this living body are full of other living bodies, plants and animals, each one of which also has its own substantial form, or dominant monad. (§§66–70)

Efficient versus final causation

It was not enough for Leibniz merely to assert that there was a correspondence between monads and the material world of phenomena. He had also to explain *how* they mapped off against each other. His answer can best be understood through his resolution of the dispute as to whether or not nature was purposeful – in traditional terms, whether or not there were *final* as well as mechanical or *efficient* causes.

Leibniz's compromise between those who rigidly excluded final causes from nature, and those who made them central to it, consisted in revamping the traditional view that all events have *both* efficient *and* final causes. In terms of his philosophy, they have efficient causes when considered as events in the material world, and final causes when considered as changes in the perceptions of monads. The best example is that of human behaviour, since it is the only case in which we are directly aware of the spiritual as well as of the bodily dimension. By introspection we know our own purposes and intentions, and can make sense of the development of our personalities in terms of a rational progression of final causes. Parallel to this, we could in theory discover a purely material causal network fully determining our behaviour – genes, environment, brain-states and so on. Far from being incompatible with each other, Leibniz believed that the two types of explanation were mutually indispensable. However, before we see how they interlocked, we must first distinguish two different levels at which Leibniz believed final causes to operate.

At the level of the individual monad, finality is essential to its internal principle of activity. In higher monads, it finds expression in conscious desires and purposes; in lower ones, it is simply an unconscious motivation (or 'appetition', as Leibniz called it) towards a better state. An alternative way of seeing it is as the driving force behind the progressive

actualisation of the monad's complete concept as determined by God. So to explain one of its states in terms of final causes is to show how this state contributes towards the perfection of the whole. However, the whole is nothing other than the totality of its perceptions, which, as we have seen, is an expression of the *material* universe. So, since matter is the province of *efficient* causation, there is now the problem of preventing final causes from collapsing into efficient ones. I shall come back to this shortly.

The other level at which finality operates is that of the universe as a whole. Given that the universe was created by a perfect and omnipotent God, it must be the best possible, at least taken over its whole history. If it is still imperfect, it must be advancing towards better and better states. This thesis is generally known as the *Principle of the Best*. But the 'best' is not just the *morally* best. Leibniz was thinking primarily of functional and aesthetic criteria, according to which the universe was the perfect product of the divine craftsman. From the functional point of view, this meant that nothing was redundant or without a sufficient reason. Aesthetically, it meant that the widest possible variety of phenomena was included under the simplest and most elegant mathematical formulae – precisely the criterion adopted by many modern philosophers of science for justifying choices between competing scientific theories that are equally compatible with the known facts. So we can now understand Leibniz's claim that mechanics depends on metaphysics: the mechanical laws which actually prevail in the universe are those that result in the best possible compromise between the conflicting requirements of variety and simplicity.

The obvious question now is: How could the independent and selfish purposes of infinitely many individual monads conspire to produce the most perfect possible whole? This was a particularly serious problem for Leibniz, in view of his denial of any real interaction between substances. His solution was his *System of Pre-Established Harmony*: although the evolution of each monad was entirely spontaneous and self-contained, God selected for creation just those possible monads that would express the maximum mutual harmony.

He illustrated his idea by an analogy of two clocks keeping perfect time with each other. There was no need to suppose that there must be some hidden connexion between their workings, nor that they were periodically adjusted. It could simply be that they were perfectly made. Likewise God, with his infinite skill, had created an infinity of monads so well that they would keep in perfect harmony to eternity.

Modern technology offers more striking examples – spaceships programmed to dock in orbit, synchronised robots in factories and so on. A better model of Leibniz's system would be an elaboration of the example of the cube (see p. 89 f.). Computer graphics can be used to create animated film sequences representing the changing shapes and positions of imaginary objects from particular perspectives. We can imagine an infinity of such films, each from infinitesimally different viewpoints, all being run simultaneously. Even though the objects and their interactions are entirely fictional, it will be *as if* there had been infinitely many cameras filming one and the same scene from different points of view. The simplest way of describing what they portrayed would be by adopting that fiction, even though its only reality would be as a formula in a computer program. But although this formula would not be *real* in the sense of having a physical embodiment outside the computer, it would be *objective*. It would be the only representation not biased towards one or other perspective, and all the others could be derived from it.

This is very much how Leibniz pictured his universe of

monads. Each monad represented a distinct point of view. Every point of view had to be taken up, otherwise an opportunity for greater variety would have been missed. No point of view could be shared by more than one monad, since the individual identity of monads depended on the precise perspective of their perceptions (see p. 56 f.). Moreover, monads could not exist without the phenomenal world of matter and efficient causation, since that world *was* their perceptions.

Finally, we must now return to the question of how Leibniz managed to preserve a distinction between active, purposeful perceivers, and passive, mechanically determined matter, given that they both ultimately consisted in perceptions. For this, he borrowed Descartes' terminology of 'distinct' as opposed to 'confused' ideas: a monad was active, purposeful and spiritual in so far as its perceptions were distinct; and passive, mechanically determined and material in so far as they were confused. The language is highly metaphorical. What he actually meant was that, even though both sorts of cause always operate, the final cause is primary when an agent's state follows most naturally from the previous states of its *own* body; and the efficient cause is primary when it follows most naturally from the previous states of surrounding bodies.

For example, if I steal up on someone and hit him on the head, his perception of the event will be one of shock and confusion, whereas I will have had a distinct and orderly progression of perceptions culminating in the intended action. Anyone who wanted to explain what had happened to the other person would do so more naturally by reference to what was going on in *me* immediately beforehand, even though it would in theory be possible to unravel the relevant information from the victim's confused 'little perceptions'. As Leibniz himself wrote in the *Monadology*:

Created things are said to be *active* in proportion to their degree of perfection, and to be *passive* with respect to others in proportion to their imperfection. Thus *activity* is attributed to monads in so far as their perceptions are distinct, and *passivity* in so far as they are confused. And one creature is more perfect than another if it provides the *a priori* reason for what happens in the other; and that is how it is said to act on it. But among simple substances, the influence of one monad on another is only *ideal* . . . That is why activity and passivity are mutual among created things. For God, comparing two simple substances, finds in each one reasons which oblige him to accommodate the other to it, and, consequently, that which is active in certain respects, is passive from another point of view: *active* in so far as what is known distinctly in it supplies the reason for what happens in another, and *passive* in so far as the reason for what happens in it is found in what is known distinctly in another. (§§49–52)

In short, there exist only monads, and monads are nothing other than actualised sets of perceptions defined by a particular point of view. Every perception is both spontaneous (arising from the essence of the individual monad) and harmonious (adapted to the rich pattern of the whole universe). Form and matter represent these two complementary aspects. A monad is a form or spirit in so far as it is spontaneous, active and purposeful; it belongs to the realm of material bodies in so far as it is accommodated to the actions of other substances through the laws of mechanics. For all created beings, the bodily dimension is inescapable. Without it, they would be wholly active and perfect, which is a privilege reserved for God alone.

6 God and man

Mysticism

Leibniz's metaphysical account of the difference between God and the world had both mystical and moral repercussions. We have just seen how he held that the created universe was distinct from God in virtue of its passive, material and mechanistic aspect. But if matter is unreal, this means that the materiality of the world consists in an admixture of unreality, or not-being. God is pure being: matter is a compound of being and nothingness (S ii 411).

Leibniz elevated this into what he called a 'mystical theology', by taking up two of the principal ideas of Pythagoras, and adding one of his own. Pythagoras believed both that numbers were the ultimate realities, and that the universe as a whole was harmonious, in that it manifested simple mathematical ratios, like those of the basic intervals in music (the 'harmony of the spheres'). Leibniz accepted both these positions. His novel contribution was to make the numbers *binary*. Just as the whole of arithmetic·could be derived from 1 and 0, so the whole universe was generated out of pure being (God) and nothingness. God's creative act was therefore at one and the same time a voluntary dilution of his own essence, and a mathematical computation of the most perfect number derivable from combinations of 1 and 0. Binary arithmetic was not merely a convenient notation for the hierarchy of all possible concepts, but it was the most faithful possible way of representing their very essence, with 1 and 0 themselves functioning as the only absolutely simple concepts. As Leibniz himself wrote, probably as early as his Paris period:

Perhaps only one thing is conceived independently, namely God himself – and also nothing, or absence of being. This can be made clear by a superb analogy . . . [He then outlines the binary system, and continues:] I shall not here go into the immense usefulness of this system; it would be enough to note how wonderfully all numbers are thus expressed by means of Unity and Nothing. But although there is no hope in this life of people being able to arrive at the secret ordering of things which would make it evident how everything arises from pure being and nothingness, yet it is enough for the analysis of ideas to be continued as far as is necessary for the demonstration of truths. (C 430–1)

Leibniz was so proud of this idea, that he planned to commemorate it with a medal bearing the legends: THE MODEL OF CREATION DISCOVERED BY G.W.L., and ONE IS ENOUGH FOR DERIVING EVERYTHING FROM NOTHING. His design emphasised his debt to Pythagoras and Plato, in depicting the sun, or 1, radiating its light on formless earth, or 0. The theme of sun and light also occurs elsewhere. For instance, *On the True Mystical Theology* (S ii 410–13) is centred round a dualism of the worlds of light and of shadows; and in the *Monadology* he writes:

So God alone is the primitive unity, or original simple substance, of which all created or derivative monads are products. They are, so to speak, born from moment to moment through continual flashes of divine light, up to the capacity of the created substance, which is of its very nature limited. (§47)

Theodicy

The ethical counterpart of the doctrine that the world is differentiated from God by the inclusion of not-being, is that the element of not-being explains why the world must be morally less perfect than its creator. It provided Leibniz with a solution to the age-old Problem of Evil, namely the problem of how to reconcile God's goodness and omnipotence with the existence of evil in the world. He made this the central theme of the only full-scale philosophical work he published, namely the *Theodicy* (or vindication of the justice of God) of 1710. His main target was Pierre Bayle (1647–1706), the French sceptic and encyclopaedist. Bayle had held that religious belief could only depend on faith, on the grounds that insoluble problems such as that of the existence of evil meant that Christianity was contrary to reason.

A primitive solution to the problem had been to ascribe evil to a rival power, but from the first few centuries of the Christian era this had been outlawed as the heresy of Manicheism (after the third-century Eastern heretic, Manichaeus, who held that good and evil were equal principles). St Augustine, the great extirpator of Manicheism, had tried to get round the difficulty by appealing to the Platonic idea that evil is only a privation. If it was an absence of goodness rather than anything positive in itself, then it would require no special apology. Leibniz agreed that evil was not some real force opposed to God's goodness. On the other hand, he saw that even if evil were nothing other than an absence of goodness, it still seemed to be incompatible with God's perfection.

Leibniz's solution had two parts. The first was to admit that the universe was indeed imperfect, but to point out that its imperfection was logically necessary in order to preserve its distinctness from God, the only perfect being. God could not be blamed for failing to contravene the laws of logic. The other part of his answer was to say that, although the universe was not perfect, it was the *best possible* – it was as perfect as it could be without collapsing back into God himself. Consequently, to blame God for creating this universe as he did would be tantamount to saying that he should not have created anything at all.

The trouble with Leibniz's solution to the problem was that, although it may have been theologically sound, it seemed to fly in the face of common-sense experience of natural disasters, misery, disease, cruelty, poverty and so on. Indeed, many people would regard Leibniz's optimism as not merely false in point of fact. but outrageously and wickedly complacent. One person to take this attitude was Voltaire, who bitterly satirised Leibniz as Dr Pangloss (who 'glossed over everything'), in his novel *Candide*.

Leibniz himself was well aware of the objection, and tried to forestall it by focusing on a separate logical limitation to the possibility of a perfect world. This was not that the world could not be better without becoming *God*, but that it could not be better without becoming *worse*. That is, the elimination of what might seem a fault from one perspective, would constitute a greater evil from other points of view.

To give a few examples: At the moral level, our personalities would be diminished if there were no possibility of sin, or no temptations to overcome. At the level of nature, the absence of disasters and discomforts would require such irregularities in causal laws as to preclude the possibility of science and engineering. At the aesthetic level, we should not judge a whole from a tiny portion. Looked at too closely, a part of a painting will seem to be an ugly and meaningless jumble of pigment. Similarly, a chord in a piece of music may be a cacophonous discord in itself, but crucial for the harmony of the whole.

So, whatever might be said about how imperfect the world in fact is, Leibniz can always produce some account of how this is compatible with its being the best possible. But he is thereby vulnerable to a different objection, namely that his thesis is meaningless, in that nothing could count as evidence against it. Leibniz himself had made just the same point against Descartes. Descartes had maintained that it would detract from God's omnipotence if moral values were not subject to his will, and concluded that the sole criterion for what was good must be that which God had willed to bring about. But, as Leibniz saw, it then became meaningless to describe God himself as good, since nothing could count as an evil action willed by God. Even if he did everything that the Devil is supposed to have done, it would still be good, as having been willed by God. In the case of Leibniz's God, the infinity of the universe meant that the reserves of possible counterbalancing factors could always outweigh any empirical evidence that the universe was worse than it could have been. Consequently, it would seem that his thesis that this is the best of all possible worlds is equally vacuous.

At the purely moral level, this is probably fair comment. Leibniz does not propose any set of moral values by which we can judge the actual world. So far his position is, like Descartes', the basically Stoic one, that whatever actually happens must be for the best, as ordained by Providence. But at the aesthetic level, Leibniz does have perfectly clear criteria for what the perfection of the world consists in, and how it could have been worse. For instance, it would have been worse if it had not been amenable to description in terms of elegant causal laws – and in this case, any local irregularities could not be explained away as contributing to the greater harmony of the whole.

Man's place in nature

Leibniz had objected to Descartes' taking the human soul right out of nature. But he himself was prone to the opposite danger of understating the differences between man and everything else. He certainly agreed with earlier philosophers that man (or rather, man and other superior spirits) was distinguished from animals by possessing both consciousness and reason. But he also held that most of the factors determining our behaviour were *un*conscious; and that most of our reasoning was *ad hoc* and instinctive, rather than abstract and rational. In practice, man normally differed from other animals only in the degree of complexity of his behaviour, and not in kind. The other traditional distinguishing mark was man's possession of an immortal soul. But here too Leibniz was in a difficulty, since he held that *all* animals, indeed all genuine substances whatever, had souls by virtue of being organic, and that these souls were indestructible by virtue of being simple. As he wrote in the *Monadology*:

There is also no fear of dissolution, and there is no conceivable way for a simple substance to die in the natural course of events – nor for one to come into being, since it could not be formed by a process of construction. So you can say that monads can only come in and out of being abruptly, that is by creation or annihilation; as contrasted with compounds, which come in or out of being bit by bit. (§§4–6)

Leibniz concluded that birth was only a 'growth and development', and death only an 'envelopment and diminution' (*Monadology*, § 73), so that there was both pre-existence and survival on this earth after death. He was well aware of his closeness to Pythagoras' belief in the transmigration of human and animal souls:

I have the highest opinion of Pythagoras, and I almost believe that he was superior to all other ancient philosophers, since he virtually founded not only mathematics, but also the science of incorporeals, having formulated that famous doctrine, worthy of a whole hecatomb, that all souls are immortal. (G vii 497)

Whether or not it would have been appropriate to celebrate this particular discovery with the slaughter of a hundred oxen, it is important not to interpret Leibniz as being more Pythagorean than he really was. There are two major respects in which their theories of pre-existence and survival were radically different.

The first difference is that Pythagoras held that souls migrated from one body to another, whereas Leibniz maintained that a soul, as the form of its body, could not become attached to any body other than its original one. It is true that he did picture the soul as animating a minute animalcule pre-existing in the seed of the parent, and as remaining alive, once more as an animalcule, after the death of the animal it had grown into – rather as a king might survive the dissolution of the state he once ruled. But Leibniz's essential point was not far removed from modern biology. If a monad was a concentration of information about its organic body, and the organism itself was a larger or smaller embodiment of that information, then he was saying that animal bodies included organic components which embodied the information required for generating future unborn individuals – in other words, genetic codes. In a manner of speaking, monads were gonads. But the more radical thesis that genetic information could never be lost (an aspect of his 'principle of the conservation of information') was much wider of the mark.

The other difference between Leibniz and Pythagoras is that the Pythagorean theory was utterly heretical for a Christian. So Leibniz claimed that our special status as human beings exempted us from the cycle of rebirth. As mere biological entities, our organic bodies with their corresponding souls existed before and after this life. But it was an entirely separate question whether or not the souls always had human status.

At one level, human status consisted simply in the capacity for self-consciousness and reason. Leibniz maintained that human souls were miraculously elevated to this status on conception, but he refused to speculate on what might happen to us after death. This was no doubt politic, since his philosophy had no room for the idea of any complete escape from the material world through some special act of Divine Grace. All substances had to have bodies, and thereby belong to this world – even angels.

At another level, Leibniz identified our humanity, not with our inner nature or capacities, but with a special *moral* status. Adapting Augustine's idea of a 'City of God', he distinguished between the realms of *Nature* and of *Grace*. All sub-human creatures belong only to the Realm of Nature; but we have the privilege of dual nationality, and are also citizens of the Realm of Grace. As such, we enter into a special set of relationships with God. We are not merely natural machines created by the Author of Nature, but we are the subjects of the Heavenly King. As such we have all sorts of privileges and duties that mere animals lack, and it is these that ultimately constitute our human status.

Leibniz's account side-steps many of the philosophical difficulties with other theories of what it is to be human. However, it only makes sense if he can explain how our status as moral agents is compatible with our being at the same time subject to the deterministic laws of nature.

Freedom and determinism

Along with the problem of the composition of the continuum, that of freedom and determinism was one of the 'two great labyrinths in which our reason very often gets lost' (G vi 29). As usual, Leibniz aimed for a compromise between two extreme positions, each of which had part of the truth. The extremes were *fatalism* and *indeterminism*. He held that fatalists were wrong to deny the practical and moral significance of human action, and that indeterminists were wrong to deny that human behaviour was causally determined and in principle predictable. Leibniz was what is now known as a 'compatibilist', holding that freedom and determinism were compatible with each other.

He identified two main forms of fatalism. The first was what he called *Muhammadan* fatalism. The Muhammadan form consisted in arguing that there was no point in trying to achieve or avoid anything, since God would in any case bring about what he had willed, whatever we might do. Leibniz rejected the argument on the grounds that it separated men's actions from God's plan for the universe. He saw human behaviour as wholly embedded within the deterministic scheme of things, and hence as playing an essential role in the fulfilment of the divine plan. The plan was not carried out *despite* human volitions and actions, but *through* them. In effect, the Muhammadan position erred in being indeterminist as well as fatalist, since it assumed that God might miraculously interfere with the normal course of nature in order to play cat and mouse with us.

A more purely philosophical version of fatalism denied that our actions could influence the future, on the grounds that everything that happened in the world was *logically necessitated*. Descartes, Hobbes and Spinoza all tended towards this position. Leibniz diagnosed their error as arising from a failure to distinguish between physical and logical necessity. This was partly a consequence of their seeing physics as nothing other than geometry with an added fourth dimension of time. The history of the universe consisted in the unfolding through time of all possible geometrical configurations of matter, so that every possibility would be actualised at some time or other. There was therefore no room for the notion of a genuine possibility which could be either brought about or prevented by human action.

As we saw earlier (p. 59), Leibniz defined the logically

necessary as that of which the opposite implies a contra-diction, and held that different states of affairs were actualisations of different sets of logically discrete predicates. Since the presence or absence of any particular predicate would make no difference to the logical consistency of the rest, this meant that the opposite of a given state of affairs could *never* imply a contradiction. There must therefore be an infinity of possibilities which never have been, and never will be actualised.

All the same, there is still a certain inevitability about the operations of the laws of nature. Leibniz described this as 'moral', or 'physical' necessity, as opposed to 'logical', 'math-ematical' or 'metaphysical' necessity. Sometimes, in order to soften the impact of his determinism, he adapted the astro-logical tag 'The stars incline without necessitating', and said that we are only 'inclined', and not necessitated by the laws of nature. But this was no more than a rhetorical device, since we are no more capable of performing *physically* impossible actions than we are of *logically* impossible ones. Merely to have shown that we are not *logically* fated does not of itself explain how our freedom is compatible with determinism.

As for indeterminism, Leibniz thought it was wrong on two counts. The first was that it was incompatible with the Princi-ple of Sufficient Reason to suppose that God could have stayed his hand from determining every detail of the universe during the act of creation. If he had left anything to the discretion of his creatures, the resultant history of the uni-verse could only have been worse than the best possible.

His second argument was that what he called a 'freedom of indifference' would in any case be of no benefit. If a free action was one that could not be attributed to your character, ambi-tions, appreciation of the environment and so on, then that would make it an absurd and irrational whim – quite the opposite of morally responsible behaviour. Indeed, a piece of behaviour not determined by your past history would not be *your* action at all. An action is yours solely in virtue of the way it fits into the total pattern of your life, and an essentially unpredictable decision would count as a passion, or something that happens to you, rather than as an action. Given also that causal determinism is nothing other than conformity with the pattern of a system as a whole, your being caught up in the deterministic system is the price you have to pay for being an active agent at all (see pp. 86–7, 99).

If Leibniz had been an atheist, he could have left it at that, and said that it makes no sense to want more freedom than we already have. We are not imposed upon by external forces, such as past history or the influence of our environment, since we *are* the most immediate of those forces. There is no 'us' over and above the sum of our previous experiences to be determined by those experiences. But Leibniz did have the problem of explaining how we could escape being mere puppets of *God*.

He attempted to solve the problem by means of his doctrine that a person's essence was his complete concept in the mind of God. He argued that complete concepts were not determined by God, since God merely reviewed all the logically possible permutations and combinations of predicates. In creating a person, he selected one of many possible complete concepts for actualisation, and the process of actualisation changed nothing in the concept. In particular, it could not add any element of necessity or divine determination linking its predicates together. The succession of predicates was as free and random in reality as it was in the original coming together of the concept.

Taken at face value, Leibniz's solution is completely inadequate. From our point of view as actually existent

111

individuals, the course of our lives is still wholly determined by God. It may be that God did no more than select the blueprints of our future histories from the infinity of logical possibilities, but it remains the case that his choice uniquely determines what happens to us. Besides, Leibniz's account applies equally to all monads, and therefore cannot explain the special status of human freedom and moral responsibility.

However, it is likely that his remarks were intended only as a piece of philosophical diplomacy. For the benefit of anyone worried by the idea of necessitation, he stresses that we each have an infinite variety of logically possible futures. But the fact that we are no *more* free than animals or material objects, means that we have no special privilege of freedom granted by God. Leibniz is therefore committed to the Stoic position that all is predestined by Providence: rather than undergo the stress and frustration of struggling against the inevitable, we should apply our Reason to the task of aligning our perspectives on the world with the optimal perspective that God has. We have not been endowed with a miraculous freedom, but God has at least granted us the gift of Philosophy, which enables us to understand how all is ultimately for the best in the best of all possible worlds.

7 Influence

Leibniz's most immediate influence was as a mathematician. In particular, Continental mathematicians adopted his version of the infinitesimal calculus in preference to Newton's – a fact which opened up a divide between British and Continental science which was to take over a century to heal. His philosophical influence was rather less direct, but such as it was, it helped to widen the gulf still further. His principal disciple was Johann Christian Wolff (1679–1754), whose philosophy was dominant in Germany for most of the eighteenth century, and had a considerable influence on Kant. Leibniz's tendencies towards speculation and system-building found an exaggerated expression in Wolff's work, and still constitute a major point of difference between the styles of Continental and English-language philosophy, which has always preferred the more empiricist and *ad hoc* approach deriving from Bacon, Hobbes and Locke.

It is ironical that one so devoted to the cause of mutual understanding should have succeeded only in adding to intellectual chauvinism and dogmatism. There is a similar irony in the fact that he was one of the last great polymaths – not in the frivolous sense of having a wide general knowledge, but in the deeper sense of one who is a citizen of the whole world of intellectual inquiry. He deliberately ignored boundaries between different disciplines, and lack of qualifications never deterred him from contributing fresh insights to established specialisms. Indeed, one of the reasons why he was so hostile to universities as institutions was because their rigid faculty structure prevented the cross-fertilisation of ideas which he saw as essential to the advance both of knowledge and of wisdom. The irony is that he was himself instrumental in bringing about an era of far greater intellectual and scientific specialisation, as technical advances pushed more and more disciplines out of the reach of the intelligent layman and amateur.

It is difficult not to be impressed by the number of ways in which Leibniz's ideas were far ahead of his time. But his being out of his time made him all the less influential. Generally, it has only been after the independent rediscovery of his ideas that his priority has been noticed. For example, the mathematician and logician, George Boole (1815–64), had first to reinvent the idea of mathematical logic for the chief architects of modern logic, Gottlob Frege (1848–1925) and Bertrand Russell (1872–1970) to appreciate that Leibniz was a fellow spirit. On the other hand, re-evaluation can also go too far. Thus followers of the current fashion for 'possible worlds logic' (according to which necessary truths are necessary because they are true in all possible worlds) have tried to father their approach on Leibniz, even though his concept of a possible world was radically different from theirs.

Leibniz's greatness as a philosopher did not consist just in his ability to back winners. If that had been so, the task of the scholar would merely be to search among his quaint and outmoded ideas, in order to 'salvage' those that anticipate modern beliefs. But this would be an arrogant and patronising attitude to adopt to one of the best minds in the history of philosophy. If we are to treat Leibniz as the master he was, we must be prepared to follow his lead.

But what example was Leibniz setting? As we have seen, in content his philosophy was largely an updating of the Pythagorean and Platonic traditions, using the concepts of Aristotelian scholasticism. In style and spirit, however, he was very much a Socrates. He was always in dialogue with others, trying to sympathise with a variety of different points of view, but ready to turn into a philosophical gadfly with professionals, specialists and experts who assumed that they had the whole of the truth on any question. It is easy to advocate following in the Socratic tradition, but few have followed it as successfully as Leibniz.

Further reading

Biography

The principal sources for Leibniz's biography are: G. E. Guhrauer, *Gottfried Wilhelm, Freiherr von Leibniz: Eine Biographie*, 2 vols (Breslau, 1842), and K. Müller and G. Krönert, *Leben und Werk von G. W. Leibniz: Eine Chronik* (Frankfurt am Main, 1969). The only biography in English is E. J. Aiton's *Leibniz: A Biography* (Bristol, 1985). This work also includes clear and detailed expositions of Leibniz's principal ideas.

Translations

Only a small proportion of Leibniz's writings is available in English. By far the most comprehensive selection is *Philosophical Papers and Letters*, ed. Leroy E. Loemker, 2nd ed. (Dordrecht, 1969). Useful smaller selections are: *Discourse on Metaphysics, Correspondence with Arnauld, and Monadology*, ed. G. R. W. Montgomery (Chicago, 1902, reprinted 1980), *Philosophical Writings*, ed. G. H. R. Parkinson (London, 1973), *Leibniz Selections*, ed. P. P. Wiener (New York, 1951), and *Logical Papers: A Selection*, trans. G. H. R. Parkinson (Oxford, 1966). Manchester University Press have published very helpful editions of *The Discourse on Metaphysics* (1953), *The Leibniz-Arnauld Correspondence* (1967), and *The Leibniz-Clarke Correspondence* (1956). There is also a translation of the *Theodicy* by E. M. Huggard (London, 1952), and of the *New Essays* by P. Remnant and J. Bennett (Cambridge, 1981; abridged, 1982).

Commentaries

In comparison with other major philosophers, there are relatively few commentaries on Leibniz in English. Two of the most accessible works happen to be posthumously edited lecture courses from Oxford and Cambridge: H. W. B. Joseph's *Lectures on the Philosophy of Leibniz*, ed. J. L. Austin (Oxford, 1949; reprinted, 1973), and C. D. Broad's *Leibniz: An Introduction*, ed. C. Lewy (Cambridge, 1975). Other elementary introductions are N. Rescher's *Leibniz: An Introduction to his Philosophy* (Oxford, 1979), and S. Brown's *Philosophers in Context: Leibniz* (Brighton, 1983). Bertrand Russell's *A Critical Exposition of the Philosophy of Leibniz* (Cambridge, 1900) is of central importance in the history of Leibniz scholarship, but it is difficult, and rather unbalanced in approach. There are a number of useful collections of articles, such as *Leibniz: A Collection of Critical Essays*, ed. H. G. Frankfurt (Notre Dame, 1976), and *Leibniz: Metaphysics and Philosophy of Science*, ed. R. S. Woolhouse (Oxford, 1981). For Leibniz's mathematical development, there is an excellent translation of J. E. Hofmann's *Leibniz in Paris (1672–1676)* (Cambridge, 1974), and for his logic, there is G. H. R. Parkinson's *Logic and Reality in Leibniz's Metaphysics* (Oxford, 1965). G. Buchdahl's *Metaphysics and the Philosophy of Science* (Oxford, 1969) contains a valuable chapter on the relation between Leibniz's science and his metaphysics; the dispute with the Newtonians is clearly and comprehensively treated in A. R. Hall's *Philosophers at War: The Quarrel between Newton and Leibniz* (Cambridge, 1980); and his ethics in J. Hostler's *Leibniz's Moral Philosophy* (London, 1975). All these books contain more or less extensive bibliographies; but for a really complete bibliography one must refer to K. Müller, *Leibniz-Bibliographie: Verzeichnis der Literatur über Leibniz* (Frankfurt am Main, 1967).

Index

activity, 43–4, 87, 93, 96, 99–100, 110–11
alchemy, 5, 15–16
Alsted, J. H., 7
analyticity, 58–61
Anton Ulrich, Duke, 18, 20–1
Aristotle, 3, 51–2, 61, 63
Arnauld, A., 11, 58, 85
atomism, 1, 56, 77–84, 89, 95
Augustine, St, 103, 108

Bacon, F., 50, 76, 113
Bayle, P., 103
Becher, J. J., 15–16
Bernoulli, J., 70
best, principle of the, 85, 97, 103–5, 110, 112
binary arithmetic, 29–30, 66, 71–2, 101–2
Boineburg, Baron J. C. von, 5–13
Boineburg, P. W., 12–13
Boole, G., 71, 114
Boscovich, R. G., 44
Brand, H., 16
Burchard, J., 20

calculator, 12–13, 30, 63, 66, 69, 72
calculus, infinitesimal, 30–6, 113
Caramuel y Lobkowitz, J., 29–30
Catholicism, 6, 24, 27, 78
causes, efficient and final, 96–100
characteristic, universal, 13, 61–6
China, 9, 12, 29
church unity, 6, 18
circle, squaring the, 33–4
Clarke, S., 25, 44, 46, 56
classes, 51, 68–70, 72

coach design, 15–16, 19
cohesion, 78–82
combinatoric, 4, 61, 66, 68, 101, 111
compounds, 53–5, 89
concepts, simple and complex, 51–2, 63–6, 68–70, 101
concepts, complete, 57–60, 68, 97, 100, 110–12
consciousness, 79, 84, 92–3, 96, 105–7
conservation, laws of, 37–40, 45–6
contingency, 58
continuity, 82–3
correspondence, 9, 19, 25, 44
Crafft, J. D., 5, 15–16

definition, 50–3, 63, 65
des Billettes, G., 75
des Bosses, B., 25, 32
Descartes, R., 1, 11, 37–9, 42, 50, 61, 76, 78–84, 90, 99, 104–5, 109
determinism, 84, 87, 95–6, 99, 108–12
dialectic, 74, 115
diplomacy, 20–4, 112
discovery, logic of, 50, 60–6
Duns Scotus, 53
dynamics, 40–4

Eckhart, J. G., 8, 26
Egypt, 11–12
Einstein, A., 47–8
elasticity, 40–3
encyclopaedia, universal, 6–7, 62
energy, 37–46, 83–4, 86, 88, 95
entropy, 44–6

Ernst August, Duke, 17–18, 20
ether, 42, 80
Euclid, 50, 61
Euler, L., 69–70
evil, problem of, 102–5
existence, problem of, 56–7, 60

fatalism, 108–10
field theory, 44, 95
fluxion, 35, 82–3, 88
form and matter, 52–3, 79, 87–8, 91, 95, 100, 107
freedom, 108–12
Frege, G., 114
Friedrich I, King of Prussia, 21–2

Galileo, 37
Gassendi, P., 77–8
Georg Ludwig, Elector, 20, 24–5
Georg Wilhelm, Duke, 18
German language, 3, 9–10
God, 37, 45, 47, 56–7, 60, 75, 85, 97–8, 100–12
grace, realm of, 108

Hariot, T., 29
harmony, 76, 86, 90–1, 97–101, 104–5
Harz mountains, 16–19
Helmont, F. M. van, 84
historical research, 17–20, 24–6
Hobbes, T., 50, 73, 76–7, 84, 109, 113
humanism, 3, 10, 50
Huygens, C., 11, 37

identity, principle of, 62, 73
immortality, 106–8
indeterminism, 108, 110–11
indiscernibles, principle of the identity of, 52–3, 56, 58, 78, 80
individuation, 53, 78, 81, 99
infinitesimals, 32
infinity, 81, 92–5

influence, 113–5
information, conservation of, 32, 46, 95, 107
interaction, 42, 85–7, 90, 93, 98–100

Jesuits, 9, 25, 27
Joan, Pope, 20
Johann Friedrich, Duke, 14, 16–18

Kant, I., 1–2, 113
Ker of Kersland, 21
kinematics, 41, 44

Latin language, 3–4, 9–10
law, 4, 6–7, 50
Leeuwenhoek, A. van, 14
Leibniz, A. C., 3
Leibniz, F., 3
Leibniz, J. F., 3
Leibniz wheel, 13
Leibniz's law, 53
Leibniz's test, 33
lenses, 13–14
librarianship, 6–8, 14–15, 18
linguistics, 19–20, 23, 54–5
Linnaeus, C., 51
Locke, J., 1, 57, 64, 74, 113
Löffler, F. S., 3
logic, 1, 3, 49–72, 114
Louis XIV, 10–12, 25
Lull, R., 63
Lutheranism, 6, 78

Malebranche, N., 11, 73
Manicheism, 103
mathematics, 4, 11–12, 28–36, 50, 77, 113
matter, 38, 43–4, 78–84, 88–9, 94–101, 108
mechanism, 2, 77, 84–7, 94, 96–7, 99–100
method, philosophical, 73–6
microscopy, 14, 93–4

Index

mining, 16–18
miracles, 45, 107, 109, 112
modern philosophy, 1, 76–8
monads, 89–91, 94–100, 102, 106–7, 112
morality, 85, 97, 102–5, 108, 110–12
motion, 37–8, 45–6, 79–80, 82–3, 86, 88
mysticism, 101–2

Napoleon, 11
necessity, 57–60, 109–12, 114
Newton, I., 5, 30–1, 34–6, 40–50, 56, 113
Nizolio, M., 10, 49

occult virtues, 41, 57, 81
Oldenburg, H., 12
organism, 84–5, 87, 91–5, 107

Papin, D., 16
Paris Academy, 8–9, 13–14, 41
Pascal, B., 11, 13
passivity, 43, 83, 87, 99–101, 111
perceptions, distinct and confused, 92–3, 99–100
perpetual motion, 45
perspectives, 47, 54, 75–6, 89–90, 94, 98–100, 104, 112, 115
Peter the Great, 12, 23, 26
phenomenalism, 88–95
pi, 33
planetary motion, 42, 45
Plato, 10, 51, 74, 88, 102–3, 114
points, mathematical, 35, 80, 82–3, 88
Porphyry, tree of, 51–2, 65
proof, 60–6
Pythagoras, 4, 101–2, 106–7, 114

Ray, J., 51
realism, 88–95
reality, 53–7, 98

relations, 53–7
Renaissance philosophy, 1, 49–50
rhetoric, 4, 49
Royal Society, 8–9, 12, 14
Rudolf August, Duke, 18
Russell, B., 74, 114

salary, 18–19, 22–4, 27
Schickard, W., 13
Schmuck, C., 3
scholasticism, 3, 41, 49–50, 53, 76–82, 87, 91, 114
Schönborn, J. P. von, 6, 13
Schönborn, M. F. von, 12
Schuller, G. H., 5
science, 37–48, 50, 97
semi-mental beings, 53–7
sensorium, 46–7
series, infinite, 32–4
silk, 23
societies, scientific, 8–9, 22–3
Socrates, 115
'some', ambiguity of, 67–9
Sophie, Electress, 21, 24, 27
Sophie Charlotte, Queen, 21–2, 27
soul, 38, 45, 84, 87, 90–1, 93, 95, 105–8
space, 46–8, 56, 78–9
species, 51–3, 58, 65, 68, 78
Spinoza, B. de, 1, 14, 50, 73, 109
spontaneity, 43, 85–7, 100
steam-engine, 16
Stoicism, 105, 112
Suárez, F., 77
subject–predicate form, 54–5, 66–9
substance, 53–4, 56–7, 65, 79, 82
succession rights, 10, 17, 20–1
sufficient reason, principle of, 73, 97, 110
Swift, D., 13
syllogism, 61, 66–8
system, 73–6, 113

theodicy, 102–5

topology, 29
transubstantiation, 6, 78
truth, 54, 57–60
truth-tables, 71–2

unconscious, the, 92–3, 96, 99, 106
universities, hostility towards, 2, 5,
    10, 49–50, 76–7, 113–15

Vatican, 6, 20

Venn diagrams, 69–70
vinculum substantiale, 78
virtuosity, 28, 113
vitalism, 1, 84–8
Voltaire, F.-M., 104

watches, 13
Weigel, E., 4
well-founded phenomena, 94
Wilkins, J., 64
Wolff, J. C., 113